First
dictionary

Gallery Books are available for bulk purchase for sales
promotions and premium use. For details write or telephone
the Manager of Special Sales, W.H. Smith Publishers Inc.,
112 Madison Avenue, New York, New York 10016. (212) 532-
6600.

ISBN 0-8317-3359-4

Printed in Italy

First
dictionary

GALLERY BOOKS
An Imprint of W. H. Smith Publishers Inc.
112 Madison Avenue
New York City 10016

How to use this dictionary

First Dictionary will help you to understand what words mean and how to spell them. There will be many words that you know already, others will be new to you.

As with all dictionaries *First Dictionary* contains a long list of words that are set out in the order of the letters of the alphabet. This makes it easy for you to look them up. Naturally, you have to know your alphabet. To remind you, it runs like this:
a b c d e f g h i j k l m n o p q r s t u v w x y z.

Suppose you wanted to look up the word **horse**. First you find all the words beginning with H (after the Gs and before the Is). Then you look up the words beginning with *ho*. These come after words beginning with *hi* and before words beginning with *hu*. **Horse** comes after **hope** and before **hose**. Can you see why? The alphabet runs: ...n o p q r s t... The "r" in **horse** comes after the "p" in **hope** and before the "s" in **hose**. See if can work out why **shell** comes before **shine**.

Black words
To make it easier to find the words you want to look up they are printed in heavy black letters like this:

cook

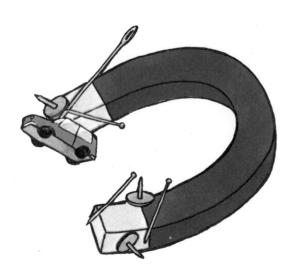

Under each word like this you will find out what the word means. If you chose, for example, the word **caterpillar**, on the next line you would see that "A **caterpillar** hatches from the egg of a moth or a butterfly." This is followed by a sentence: "**Caterpillars** crawl on plants, chewing their leaves." This gives you another form of the word caterpillar—with an "s" at the end, which we use when we want to talk about more than one caterpillar. Suppose you don't know what the word "moth" means. Look the word up and you'll see that "A **moth** is an insect that looks like a butterfly."

In the "definition" you will find the word you are looking up repeated in either the same or a different form. This is to help you to see how words change when they are used in different ways. Here is an example:

do

To **do** something means to carry out an action. Will you **do** your homework? Yes, I am **doing** it now. I **did** the work properly even if you think I **didn't**. We have **done** a lot of work today.

How to speak words

You may not know how to say some of the words. You can't "pronounce" them. How do you say the word *ballet*? You will see it rhymes with *bay* and not with *bet* because after the word there is a "pronunciation" guide: (bal-ay).

Some words are spelled the same but have different meanings. If you look up the word **capital** you will see that its first meaning (following the number 1) is: "the most important city of a country." The second meaning (following the number 2) is: "a capital letter such as B."

Use this dictionary as much as you can and have fun learning more and more about our language.

A a

A is the first letter of the alphabet. When it comes before the name of a thing it means one. I have **a** ball. You have two.

abacus

A frame with beads that move up and down on rods is called an **abacus**. An **abacus** helps you to add, subtract, multiply, or divide. In China, people have used the **abacus** for thousands of years.

about

Tell me **about** the party means say what happened. John ate **about** ten cakes means roughly that number. Walking **about** the garden means going all around it.

above

Anything higher than something else is **above** it. The roof is **above** our heads.

abroad

People go **abroad** when they leave their own country. Did you go **abroad** for your vacation?

accident (ax-id-ent)

An **accident** happens by chance. It is not expected. The cat ran across the road and caused a nasty **accident**.

The car has had an **accident**.

ache (ake)

An **ache** is a pain that goes on and on. When you have **toothache** you go to the dentist.

acrobat

An **acrobat** is a gymnast. Circus **acrobats** do tumbling and balancing tricks.

across

The girl helped a blind man **across** the road. They walked to the other side.

add

You can count how many things you have if you **add** them up. Two **added** to six equals eight. What do these numbers **add** up to: $3 + 4 + 3 = ?$

address

Your **address** is where you live. Your name and **address** are on the letters that the mailman delivers to your home.

admire

We **admire** people or things we think well of. We **admire** lifeboat crews who go out in stormy seas.

adult

An **adult** is a grown-up person. **Adults** pay full fare; children's tickets are half-price.

adventure

An **adventure** is an exciting happening. My book is about pirates who have lots of **adventures**.

advertisement

An **advertisement** is a message about something for sale. Goods for sale are **advertised** in newspapers and on television.

afford

If you have enough money you can **afford** to buy things. How can you **afford** such an expensive car?

afraid

My brother is **afraid** of spiders. They don't frighten me.

after

After means coming later. I went to bed **after** nine o'clock. John came **after** Jane in the race.

afternoon

Noon is twelve o'clock midday. The time after midday and before evening is the **afternoon**. We'll go to the zoo this **afternoon**.

again

Doing something once more means doing it **again**. We did not win the game today, but we'll try **again**.

age

1. Your **age** tells how old you are. Yesterday was my ninth birthday. My **age** is nine.
2. Some periods in history are called **Ages**. Hunters used flint knives in the Stone **Age**.

ago

What happened in the past was some time **ago**. A few minutes **ago** I did not know what **ago** meant!

agree

I **agree** with people who think the same as me. Today everyone **agrees** that the earth is round.

ahead

Ahead means in front. You go ahead and get home before me.

air

All round us is the gas called **air**. We breathe **air** to keep us alive. Birds fly through the **air**.

airplane

A flying machine with engines is an **airplane**. Pilots fly **airplanes** from one airport to another.

airport

Aircraft land and take off from an **airport**.

Airplanes take off and land at **airports**. The airplanes taxi to the runways.

album

Photos or stamps can be fixed to the empty pages of a book called an **album**. A record **album** is a collection of music on a disc.

alike

Things are **alike** when they are much the same. Tom and Nick are **alike**. They are twins.

alive

Anything which has life is **alive**. Plants and animals are **alive**. When they stop living they will be dead.

all

All is everything and everybody. Are we **all** here? Have you got **all** your books? 'All things bright and beautiful'.

alligator

An **alligator** is an animal with scaly skin, a long tail, and big jaws with sharp teeth. **Alligators** live in rivers and sunbathe on dry land.

This **alligator** has an aching tooth.

allow

If you let a friend use your pencil, you **allow** them to do it. Are you **allowed** to watch television late at night?

aloud

If you read this word **aloud** then people will hear it. Say it out loud.

alphabet

The **alphabet** has all the letters we use to make words. There are twenty-six letters in the **alphabet**. The first is "a" and the last is "z". Each letter stands for a different sound.

also

Also means as well. Today we go swimming and we **also** went on Monday.

always

John is **always** late. The sky is **always** dark at night. **Always** means all the time.

amaze

The magician's tricks **amaze** us. His **amazing** skill is always a surprise. The children were **amazed** by his magic.

ambulance

An **ambulance** takes sick people to the hospital. It has a cross on the side. It drives fast in an emergency.

The **ambulance** rushes to the accident.

American

An **American** comes from the United States of America. People who were born in America and some who live there are **American** citizens.

amount

The **amount** of money in my piggybank is very small. **Amount** means the full total. It also means number. Large **amounts** of coins are heavy to carry.

amuse

This book of jokes will **amuse** you. It made me laugh and smile. Tell me if you think it is **amusing**. **Amuse** means to entertain.

an

Words that begin with a, e, i, o, or u (like adult or egg), have "**an**" instead of "a" before them to mean "one." I always eat **an** egg for breakfast.

anchor (ank-er)

A ship's **anchor** holds it at rest. When a ship reaches harbor the heavy **anchor** is dropped into the sea and its hook digs into the seabed.

The **anchor** is on the end of a chain.

angel

The Bible tells how an **angel** gave news of Jesus's birth. **Angels** are God's messengers.

An **angel** is blowing a horn.

angry

My dad was **angry** when I broke a window. He was very annoyed indeed.

animal

An **animal** is any living thing that is not a plant. Birds, insects, and fishes are all **animals**. Worms are small **animals**. People are **animals** too.

ankle

Your **ankle** bone is between your foot and your leg.

annoy

If you **annoy** me I shall be angry. The wasps at our picnic were very **annoying**.

answer (an-sur)

Every question has an **answer**. Is your name Tom? He **answered** yes.

ant

The **ant** is a tiny animal. It is an insect. Thousands of **ants** live in one nest.

An **ant** is amazingly small.

any

I haven't **any** clean socks and I need some. **Any** and some can mean the same.

anyone

Can **anyone** come? It doesn't matter who. **Anyone** (or **anybody**) is no special person.

anything

Is **anything** in the desk? No, there is nothing. **Anything** means something.

ape

An **ape** is an animal like a monkey. But **apes** have no tails. Gorillas and chimpanzees are **apes**.

An angry **ape** jumps up and down on the anthill.

appetite

After swimming we feel hungry. We eat a big meal because we have such a big **appetite**. The more hungry you are, the bigger is your **appetite**.

apple

The **apple** tree has fruits that are good to eat. I like round, red **apples**.

Apples are good for you.

April

April is the month of the year that comes after March and before May.

apron

I wear an **apron** over my clothes when I help in the kitchen with cooking.

The girl ties her **apron**.

arch

A doorway with a curved top is an **arch**. A railroad tunnel is a long **arch**. Bridges are often held up by **arches**.

architect (are-kee-tect)

An **architect** plans how buildings are to be made.

arm

Your **arm** begins at your shoulder and ends at your wrist. In the middle of your **arm** is your elbow. I carry a bag on my arm.

armor

Soldiers used to wear metal suits of **armor** in battle. This made it harder for swords and arrows to hurt them.

The knight is wearing **armor**. Arrows cannot harm him.

army

Soldiers join together to make an **army**. In olden days kings led their **armies** into battle.

around

This hedge goes all **around** the field. Can you see **around** the corner?

arrive

We'll reach the end of our journey when we **arrive**. They **arrived** yesterday. Jane will be **arriving** tomorrow.

arrow

An **arrow** is a thin, straight stick with a pointed end. Archers shoot **arrows** from a bow.

artist

A person who paints or draws pictures is an **artist**.

as

My bag is **as** heavy **as** yours. It weighs the same. My doll is dressed **as** a nurse.

ashamed

People feel **ashamed** after they do something wrong. They know they have behaved badly.

ask

If I **ask** you a question will you answer it?

asleep

Are you **asleep**? No I am awake. If I were **sleeping** I wouldn't answer you.

astronaut

Astronauts are people who travel in space. Some **astronauts** landed on the moon.

The **astronaut** floats in space.

athlete

An **athlete** takes part in sports. **Athletes** have to be very fit to run and jump well.

atlas

A book of maps is an **atlas**. Look in the **atlas** to see where you live.

attention

Please pay **attention** and listen to what I am saying. Soldiers stand at **attention** on parade. They listen to instructions.

August

August is the month of the year that comes after July and before September.

aunt

Aunt Jane is my mother's sister. **Aunt** Ann is my father's sister. **Aunt** Daisy is married to my uncle.

autograph

People write their names in an **autograph** book. Some famous people have written in mine.

autumn

Autumn is the season when leaves fall from the trees. **Autumn** comes after summer and before winter.

awake

Are you **awake**? Yes, I am not asleep.

ax

Woodcutters chop wood with an **ax**. An **ax** is a tool with a sharp edge and a wooden handle. You can cut down trees with an **ax**.

The **ax** is very sharp.

baboon

A **baboon** is a large kind of monkey with a long tail. **Baboons** live in Africa.

baby

A **baby** is a very young child. Small **babies** cannot walk or talk.

The **baby** is wearing a blue bonnet. He is crying.

back

You are at the **back** of the class. I am at the front. Please give me **back** my pen. My **back** aches. Let's go **back** home. Please stand **back** and let me pass.

badge

People wear a **badge** to show they belong to a club or group. I wear a scout **badge** because I am a scout.

bag

A **bag** is made to carry things. My shopping **bag** is heavy. There are lots of books in my school **bag**.

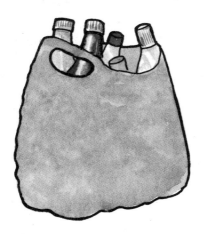

The **bag** is full of bottles. It is a green bag.

bake

We **bake** cakes in the oven. We buy bread from the **baker's** shop. The **baker bakes** bread in an oven too.

balance

The acrobat kept her **balance** when she walked the tightrope. She kept steady and did not fall.

bald

This doll has no hair. It is **bald**. Is your dad **bald**?

ball

A **ball** is round. Rubber **balls** bounce. We play ping pong with a paddle and **ball.**

She is bouncing a rubber **ball**.

ballet (bal-ay)

A **ballet** tells a story with dances and music but without words. My sister wants to be a **ballet** dancer.

balloon

A **balloon** is a bag filled with gas or air. It can float away in the sky. We blew up lots of **balloons** for my party.

Tom has a red **balloon**.

banana

A **banana** is a fruit that grows in bunches on trees. When its skin turns yellow it is ready to eat.

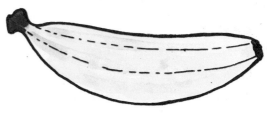

I like to peel and eat a **banana**.

band

If you play a musical instrument then you can join the **band**. Listen, the **band** is playing a march. Put this rubber **band** around your pencils to keep them together. Lucy wears a **headband** around her hair.

bandage

The doctor put a dressing on Joe's cut leg. Now he winds a **bandage** around it to keep the dressing in place. A **bandage** is a long strip of cloth.

bang

The balloon burst with a **bang**. It made a loud noise. Our baby **bangs** his toy drum.

bank

1. People keep their money in a **bank**. I keep my money at home in a **piggy-bank**.
2. The sides of a river are called **banks**.

barbecue

In summer we had a **barbecue** in the garden. We cooked our food over a fire.

bark

1. The rough, hard skin of a tree trunk is called **bark**.
2. Some dogs have a loud **bark**. Others make a yapping noise. Our dog **barks** when somebody knocks at the door.

barn

Farmers store their hay in a **barn** during the winter.

barrel

A **barrel** has curved sides and flat ends. It is made of wood and is used to store food or drink.

basket

A **basket** is made by weaving straw or twigs. It is used to carry things. My shopping **basket** is full.

bat

1. A **bat** is a small animal, like a mouse. It has a long flap of skin on both sides of its body, from neck to tail. The **bat** uses these flaps as wings. **Bats** fly at night.
2. For some games you need a **bat** to hit a ball. A cricket **bat** is thicker than a baseball **bat**. **Bats** are made of wood.

bath

I'm going to the bathroom to have a **bath**. I fill the **bathtub** with water and then climb in to wash myself all over.

Barry is having a **bubble bath**.

be

You promised to **be** good. Are you **being** good? Have you **been** good? Are you going to **be** good?
"**Be**" means "being." It is a word which can change as it is used. "**Am**," "**are**" and "**is**" are all forms of "**be**." I **am** good. You **are** good. He **is** good.
I **was** good. You **were** good. "**Was**" and "**were**" are also forms of "**be**." They show that something happened in the past.
I will **be** good tomorrow, too.

beach

The **beach** is the shore at the edge of a sea or lake. Some **beaches** are sandy. Others have pebbles.

bead

A **bead** is a small object with a hole through the middle. You can pass thread through the holes to make a string of **beads** for a necklace.

beak

The hard, pointed part of a bird's mouth is its **beak**. Birds use their **beaks** for feeding, so its shape suits the food they eat. Humming birds have long **beaks** to reach for nectar in flowers.

bean

Beans are vegetables that have seeds inside pods. Many **beans** are used for food. String **beans**, kidney **beans**, coffee **beans**, and chocolate **beans** are just a few.

bear

Bears are large wild animals. White polar **bears** live at the North Pole. Grizzly **bears** live in North America.

The **bear** lives in the forest.

beard

The hair on a man's chin and cheeks is his **beard**. Santa Claus has a curly white **beard**.

beat

1. The drummer **beat** his drum with the drumsticks. He hit it again and again.
2. That horse **beat** all the others when it came first in the race.

beaver

A **beaver** is a furry animal with a long, flat tail. It lives near water and uses branches to build dams across streams. **Beavers** make homes called lodges.

The **beavers** are building a dam.

because

I can't run **because** I have broken my leg. That is the reason why I can't run.

become

When something happens, it **becomes**. You may **become** a ballet dancer one day. It **became** dark before the storm. It is **becoming** lighter now.

bed

At night we sleep in a **bed**. We go to **bed** at **bedtime** in our **bedroom**.

I go to **bed** at seven o'clock.

bee

Bees are flying insects. They make honey and live in a **beehive**. **Bees** can sting.

The **bees** buzz around Bill's bald head.

before

1. A comes **before** F in the alphabet. Jane stood **before** the teacher. **Before** means "in front of."
2. Say goodbye **before** you go. **Before** also means earlier.

begin

We **begin** something when we start to do it. Let's **begin** at the **beginning**. We **begin** to read a book on the first page. We **began** to read the story. Have you **begun** your book yet? The movie is **beginning**.

behave

The way we act is the way we **behave**. Does your dog **behave** well?

behind

You are in front of me and I am sitting **behind** you. **Behind** means at the back of something or someone.

believe

Do you **believe** in fairies? Do you think that there are such things? Sam did not **believe** his brother. He did not think that Dick was telling the truth.

bell

A **bell** is a hollow object made of metal. It makes a ringing sound.

belong

This bag **belongs** to me. It is mine. I own this bag.

below

Below means underneath. We threw a ball out of the window to the ground **below**.

berry

A **berry** is a small fruit with seeds but no pit. I love **blackberries**, but **strawberries** are my favorite fruits. Not all **berries** are good to eat. Some are poisonous.

best

That snowman has a pipe and hat. He looks **better** than all the others. He is the **best**. I wore my **best** clothes to the party.

between

My sandwich has tomato **between** two slices of bread. **Between** means in the middle. I leave home **between** three and four o'clock.

Bible

The **Bible** tells us stories about God. It is a book that was written long ago.

bicycle

A **bicycle** has two wheels. You ride a **bike** by turning the pedals that make the wheels go round.

This is a blue **bicycle**.

big

Big things are large. The elephant was too **big** to go through the gate. A bird is **bigger** than a fly. The **biggest** animal on earth is a whale.

bill

1. The waitress gave us our **bill**. It showed how much our meal had cost. We paid the **bill** when we left the restaurant. Have you paid the telephone **bill**?
2. A bird's **bill** is its beak.

bird

A **bird** is an animal that has wings and is covered with feathers. Most **birds** use their wings to fly.

birth

The day of your **birth** is the day you were **born**. Our cat gave **birth** to six kittens.

birthday

You remember the day that your mother gave **birth** to you. Every year you have another **birthday**.

Barbara is six today. She is having a **birthday** party.

bite

Animals use their teeth to cut into things when they **bite**. Can you **bite** this hard cookie? I have **bitten** my lip.

black

Black is the darkest color. The sky at night is **black**. This pen writes with **black** ink.

blade

The sharp part of a knife or tool is the **blade**. I need a new **blade** in my pencil sharpener.

bleed

You **bleed** when you cut yourself. My knee **bled** when I fell over and the **blood** dripped on my sock.

blow

1. Take a deep breath and **blow** out the candles on your cake. **Blowing** makes the air move. The wind **blew** the leaves along.
2. A hard hit is also a **blow**. He gave the nail a hard **blow** with the hammer.

blue

Blue is the colour of the sky on a clear, sunny day.

board

A long, flat piece of wood is a **board**. This **floorboard** creaks.

boat

A **boat** floats on the water. It is a small ship.

This is a fishing **boat**. You can see the fishing nets.

body

A **body** is the whole of a person or animal. A bird's **body** is smaller than a giraffe's.

boil

Heat the water until it bubbles and steams. Then it is **boiling** hot.

bomb

Bombs are used as weapons in war. The buildings fell down when a **bomb** exploded.

bone

The hard parts of an animal's body are its **bones**. Our dog loves to gnaw a **bone**.

bonfire

Let's light a **bonfire** in the garden and burn all the trash. In the fall the park keeper makes a **bonfire** out of all the dead leaves.

The **bonfire** is burning brightly.

bongo

A **bongo** is a small drum. You can play the **bongo** drum with your fingers.

book

A **book** is made up of sheets of paper. I enjoy reading my story **book**. I write in my work **book**.

Brenda is reading a **book** about ghosts.

boot

A **boot** is a shoe that covers part of your leg as well as your foot. Put your **boots** on if it rains.

borrow

I **borrow** books from the library. I keep them for a while and then take them back. May I **borrow** a pen?

both

The two of you can go to the circus. **Both** of you can go.

bottle

A **bottle** is made for holding liquids. It is often made of glass. Pour some lemonade out of the **bottle** please.

bounce

Rubber balls **bounce**. They jump back when you throw them against something. Look at Lizzie **bouncing** on the trampoline.

bouquet (bo-kay)

A **bouquet** is a bunch of flowers. The dancers were given **bouquets** of flowers when the ballet was over.

bow (rhymes with go)

1. You can fire arrows from a long, curved piece of wood called a **bow**.
2. Ribbons are tied in **bows**. Loop the ribbon around to make a knot.
3. You can play the violin with a rod called a **bow**.
4. **Bow** (rhymes with cow) You bend over from your waist to take a **bow**. The magician **bowed** to the people and left the stage.

bowling alley

You try to knock down pins in a **bowling** alley. You stand at one end of the alley and take aim with your ball. Then you **bowl** the ball along the alley and try to knock as many pins over as possible.

box

A **box** has four straight sides and is used to store things in. Some **boxes** have a lid on top. There is a **box** full of toys in my bedroom. I keep my pencils in a cardboard **box**.

boxers

Boxers fight in a **boxing** ring. They wear big **boxing** gloves and use only their fists to fight with. We saw a **boxing** match on television. Lots of people watched the **boxers box**.

The **boxers** are boxing in the ring.

19

boy

A **boy** becomes a man when he grows up. A **boy** is a male child.

The **boy** is kicking a ball.

brain

The **brain** in your head gives commands for all the things your body does. You use your **brain** to think.

brake

The **brake** on a bicycle, car, truck, or train can make it slow down or stop. The driver put on his **brakes** when a cat ran in front of his car.

branch

A **branch** grows from the trunk of a tree. We have a tree house in the **branches** of our apple tree.

brave

The **brave** knight fought the dragon. He was not afraid. We admire his **bravery**.

bread

The **bread** we eat is made from flour and water. The baker cooks **bread** in an oven. We cut thick slices of **bread** to make toast.

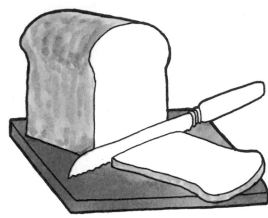

break

If you drop that cup it will **break**. Look, it has **broken** into tiny pieces. I **broke** up some bread into crumbs to feed to the birds.

breakfast

Breakfast is the first meal of the day. We have toast for **breakfast** every morning.

Betty likes a big **breakfast**.

breath

Your **breath** is the air you **breathe** in and out of your lungs. You can see your **breath** on cold, frosty days. It looks like white smoke.

brick

Lots of buildings are made of **brick**. Blocks of clay are baked hard to make **bricks**.

Bricks are used for building.

bridge

A **bridge** is built to carry people and cars across a river or a busy road.

The **bridge** is over the road.

bright

Bright things are shiny and light. The sun shines **brightly** in summer. This coin is **bright** and new.

bring

Please **bring** your work to show me. **Bring** means to carry here. My aunt **brought** me a present.

brother

My **brother** has the same mother and father as me. I am a girl. My **brother** is a boy.

brown

Brown is a dark color. Chocolate is **brown**. You can make **brown** by mixing red and yellow paint.

bruise

A **bruise** came on my leg after I bumped into a desk. A **bruise** is a black and blue patch under the skin.

brush

A **brush** is a tool made from hairs or bristles. I **brush** my teeth with a **toothbrush** and scrub my nails with a **nailbrush**. Artists use **paintbrushes** to paint their pictures.

bubble

A **bubble** is a ball of air inside a thin skin of liquid. The **bubbles** in some drinks make them fizzy.

bucket

We can carry water in a **bucket**. Hold it by the handle. **Buckets** are made of metal or plastic. I take my **bucket** and shovel to the beach. Pail is another name for a **bucket**.

The **bucket** is empty.

bud

A plant has **buds** in spring. Soon the **buds** open and grow into flowers or leaves.

build

We can put together these toy bricks and **build** a fort. The **builder built** our house with bricks, wood and cement. Our house is a new **building**.

bulb

1. Some plants grow from **bulbs** in the ground. An onion is a **bulb**. We plant **bulbs** in the autumn and they flower in spring. Daffodils grow from **bulbs**.
2. The light **bulb** glows when we switch on the electric light. We decorate the Christmas tree with tiny light **bulbs**.

bull

Cows and **bulls** are cattle. The **bull** is male and the cow is female. Male elephants and seals are also called **bulls**. Don't go into that field with the **bull**. He is very bad-tempered.

bulldozer

A **bulldozer** is a large tractor with a bucket at the front to scoop away earth. The builder used a **bulldozer** to move away a heap of earth. He **bulldozed** the building too.

The **bulldozer** bumped into the wrong building.

bump

When you **bump** something you knock against it. I **bumped** my head on the door and a **bump** came up near my eye. We had a **bumpy** ride over the field.

bunch

We picked some flowers from the garden and tied them in a **bunch**. A **bunch** is a group of things joined together. I'll have this **bunch** of bananas.

bundle

The old woman carried sticks tied in a **bundle**.

burn

A lighted match may **burn** your fingers. The cakes cooked too long and they **burned**.

burglar

A **burglar** stole silver from the house next door. We told the police about the **burglary**. Now the house has a **burglar** alarm.

burst

The red balloon **burst** with a loud bang. It exploded. The flour has **burst** out of this bag.

bury

If you **bury** something you cover it up. Pirates look for **buried** treasure. Did you **bury** the dead mouse?

The **bus** stops at the bus-stop.

bus

Lots of passengers can ride in a **bus** with plenty of seats. Some **buses** are double-deckers. People can sit on the top deck or on the bottom deck below.

bush

A woody plant that is smaller than a tree is a **bush**. Roses grow on **bushes**.

busy

I have been **busy** today. I have had a lot to do at school and at home helping Mom and Dad.

butter

I spread **butter** on my bread. **Butter** is made from cows' milk.

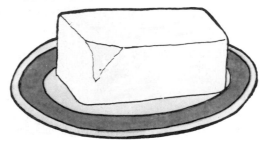

butterfly

A **butterfly** is a flying insect with large bright wings. **Butterflies** grow from caterpillars.

This **butterfly** is balanced on a blackberry.

button

A **button** is small and round. It fits into a **buttonhole** to fasten things.

buy

How many toys will my money **buy**? To **buy** that book you must pay money at the cash desk. I have **bought** a book.

by

The chair is **by** the window. It is next to it. Come **by** yourself. Will you be here **by** tomorrow?

cab

We call a **cab** when we want to ride in a taxi. The **cab** driver takes us in his car.

cabbage

A **cabbage** is a vegetable. Most **cabbages** have green leaves. My rabbit likes **cabbage**.

cactus

A **cactus** is a prickly plant. Lots of **cacti** live in deserts. They store water in their spines.

café

In the **café**, I bought a glass of milk. A **café** is a small restaurant. Some **cafés** have seats and tables in the open air.

cage

Some zoo animals are kept in **cages**. The bars of the cage stop the animals from getting out.

cake

A **cake** is made from flour, sugar, and eggs baked in the oven. **Cakes** are good to eat. I like birthday **cake**.

Carol is blowing out the candles on her **cake**.

calculator

A **calculator** is an electronic machine that can add numbers. My **calculator** helps me to do arithmetic very quickly.

calendar

A **calendar** shows us the days, weeks, and months of the year.

calf

A **calf** is a baby cow. Baby elephants, whales and seals are also known as **calves**.

call

People **call** me by my name. The lost boy **called** for help.

camel

A **camel** is a desert animal with humps on its back. Some **camels** have one hump. Other **camels** have two humps.

The **camel** is crunching a cracker.

camera

A **camera** takes photographs. With a video **camera** you can make your own TV programs.

Mike is taking pictures with his **camera**.

camp

When we stayed in a **camp** we lived in tents. I like **camping**. We **camped** in the mountains last summer.

can

1. I **can** play the piano. I am able to play a tune. I **can** also play the recorder. **Can** I go out now? Please let me.
2. In the supermarket, some foods and drinks are in metal **cans**.

Canadian

Canadians are people who come from **Canada**. **Canada** is a big country in North America.

canal

Boats float on **canals**. A **canal** carries boats inland. Be careful! The **canal** has very deep water.

candle

A **candle** is made of wax. Inside is a wick of string. **Candles** are lit on birthday cakes. I like to eat by **candlelight**.

canoe (kan-oo)

A **canoe** is a small boat, pointed at both ends. The American Indians made **canoes** of birch tree bark.

capital

1. The **capital** city of Spain is Madrid. A country is governed from its **capital** city.
2. We can write letters of the alphabet in **capitals**. Bob starts with a **capital** B, but bee does not.

captain (kap-ten)

The leader of a team is the **captain**. Jane is **captain** of the tennis team.

capture

To **capture** means to catch. The soldiers **captured** the man. He was taken **captive**.

car

The **car** is the most popular form of transportation. My **car** needs a new engine. The roads are full of **cars**.

People dress up in costumes for the **carnival**.

caravan

A **caravan** is a group of vehicles traveling together in file.

card

A **card** is a piece of thick paper with some kind of picture or writing on it. They played Old Maid with a deck of playing **cards**. I sent you a **postcard** from France.

carnival

The **carnival** parade was noisy. Everyone was dressed up. We danced in the street.

carol

At Christmas, people sing **carols**. We went **carol** singing one evening. We sang 'Silent Night', 'Away in a Manger' and 'The Holly and the Ivy'.

carpenter

The **carpenter** made these shelves. A person who works with wood making furniture or building houses, is a **carpenter**.

carpet

The floor is covered with a thick, woven **carpet** made of wool. The stair **carpet** is wearing thin.

carriage

A **carriage** was a wheeled vehicle that carried people. Harness the horses to the **carriage**, please.

carrot

A **carrot** is a root vegetable. We eat only the long orange-colored root, not the green leaves.

carry

Carry this case for me, please. A man **carried** my luggage. I held my **carry-on** bag.

cart

A **cart** is a wagon. In the olden days, horses pulled **carts** through the streets.

cartoon

I always laugh at the **cartoons** on the television. My favorite **cartoon** character is Donald Duck. The artists who draw **cartoons** are called **cartoonists**.

case

I keep my pencils in this leather **case**. My glasses have a **case** of their own to protect them.

cash

Paper money and coins are called **cash**. When you **cash** a check, the bank gives you money in exchange. With a special card, you can get **cash** from an automatic **cash** machine. You use **cash** to buy things.

castle

A **castle** is a big, stone building. People went into **castles** for safety in time of war. Most **castles** were built in the Middle Ages.

cat

Our pet **cat** likes to lie in front of the fire. It also catches birds and mice. The **cat** family includes lions, tigers, and other big **cats**.

My **cat** is very clean.

catch

1. I can **catch** a ball in one hand. **Catch** means to grab hold of something as it is moving. The angler **caught** a fish.
2. You can also **catch** or get a cold.
3. If I miss this train, I shall have to **catch** the next one.

Around the **castle** is a moat.

caterpillar

A **caterpillar** hatches from the egg of a moth or a butterfly. **Caterpillars** crawl on plants, chewing their leaves.

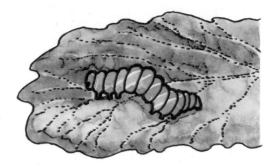

The **caterpillar** crawls across the cabbage leaf.

cattle

A **cattle** farmer keeps a herd of cows. The farmer drove the **cattle** in for milking.

cave

A **cave** is a dark hole in a mountain or underground. Exploring **caves** can be dangerous. **Cave** dwellers lived in **caves** thousands of years ago.

ceiling

My bedroom **ceiling** is painted yellow. A **ceiling** is the inside of the roof of a building.

celebrate

To **celebrate** my birthday we had a party. It was a special day. Easter is **celebrated** every year. People enjoy a **celebration**.

cell

1. Our bodies are made of tiny **cells**.
2. The prisoner was locked up in a prison **cell**.

cellar

We store wine in the **cellar** under our house.

cement mixer

The builders made cement in a **cement mixer**. The bucket goes around and around.

The **cement mixer** goes around and around.

center

The middle of something is its **center**. The **center** of a dartboard is the bullseye.

century

One hundred years is a **century** So is one humdred runs in cricket.

cereal

Cereal is my favorite breakfast. I like cornflakes. Wheat and rice are **cereals**.

chain

Rings joined together make a **chain**. In the garden, we made daisy **chains**. My bicycle **chain** needs oil. The prisoner was **chained** to the wall.

chair

A **chair** is a piece of furniture you can sit on. The king's throne is a special kind of **chair**.

champion

The **champion** is the best at anything. She won all the races and is now the **champion**.

change

To **change** means to become different. I must **change** my wet clothes. Can you give me **change** for this bill, please. He keeps **changing** his mind.

chase

To **chase** is to run after something. Let's play **chase**. We **chased** the dog when it ran out of the house. **Chasing** after it made us tired.

chatter

1. Sometimes we talk in class. We **chatter**. My friend met me and we had a **chat**.
2. My teeth are **chattering**. I am so cold, I can't stop my teeth from banging together.

cheap

A **cheap** toy does not cost a lot of money. I wanted that expensive watch, but the **cheaper** one will do.

check

Please **check** that the door is locked. I will **check** that all the windows are shut.

cheek

My **cheeks** were red after I had been running. Your **cheek** is the soft part of your face on each side of your mouth.

cheese

Cheese is a dairy food, made from milk. Blue **cheeses** have mold in them. This **cheese** smells!

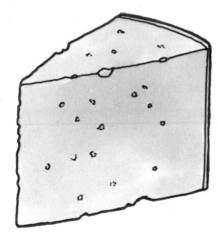

Do you like the taste of **cheese**?

cheetah

The **cheetah** is a member of the cat family. Its fur is covered with dark spots. **Cheetahs** can run faster than any other animal.

cherry

Cherry trees have round red or yellow fruits. **Cherries** are good to eat.

Three red **cherries**

chest

1. Inside your **chest** are your lungs. Your chest swells when you breathe in.
2. A **chest** is also a box for putting things in. The pirates buried their treasure in a **chest**.

chicken

Chickens are birds kept for their eggs and meat. A female **chicken** is a hen.

Sometimes we have roast **chicken**.

child

The Smiths have one **child**, a son. The Browns have three **children**, two daughters and one son. I like **children's** television.

chimney

Smoke from the fire or factory goes up a **chimney**. **Chimneys** are tall so that the smoke and gas escapes high into the sky.

chimpanzee

A **chimpanzee** is an ape. It lives in Africa. **Chimpanzees** are very intelligent animals. Baby **chimpanzees** quickly learn to do tricks.

This **chimpanzee** is chewing gum.

chin

I had to wipe my **chin** after I ate ice cream. The ice cream ran down from my mouth on to my **chin**.

china

China clay is the kind of earth from which some cups and saucers are made. The **china** teacups are pretty.

chocolate

Chocolate is a sweet food. It is made from the beans of the cacao tree. The beans are crushed into powder. Do you like **chocolate** bars?

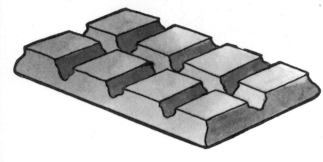

A bar of **chocolate**

Christmas

Christmas is the time when Christians celebrate the birth of Jesus Christ. We put decorations on the **Christmas** tree. It is exciting opening our **Christmas** presents.

Presents around a **Christmas** tree

church

A **church** is a building in which Christian people worship God. I went to **church** last Sunday.

circle

A **circle** is round. I drew around a coin to draw a **circle**.

circus

A **circus** is a traveling show with clowns and acrobats. A **circus** tent is called the big top.

city

A **city** is a large town. New York is the biggest **city** in The United States. Some **cities** have huge skyscrapers.

clap

I taught my baby brother to **clap**. I showed him how to beat his hands together. Everyone **clapped** in time with the music.

classroom

This is our **classroom**. We have lessons here. Our school has lots of **classrooms**.

claw

Some animals have pointed nails, or **claws** on their feet. The eagle has sharp **claws** for hunting. The cat can scratch with its **claws**. Sometimes it **claws** the furniture.

clean

I washed Dad's car to **clean** it. It was very muddy. I **cleaned** the inside too.

clear

See the fish in the pond? The water is **clear**. It is easy to see through. On a **clear** night, you can see the stars.

clever

My sister is very **clever**. She is more intelligent than I am.

cliff

From the top of the **cliff**, we could see the beach down below. The **cliffs** were very high. They rose high above the sea.

climb

To **climb** is to go up something. I **climbed** the stairs. **Climbing** the ladder was easy. **Climbing** the ropes was difficult.

Caroline is **climbing** the chestnut tree.

cloakroom

We left our coats and boots in the **cloakroom**. People used to wear **cloaks** when they went outside.

clock

A **clock** shows the time. Can you tell the time from this **clock**? It is 3 **o'clock**.

close

1. To **close** means to shut. Please **close** that door. A door that is **closed** is not open.
2. **Close** can also mean near. We live **close** to a bus stop.

cloth

Wool or cotton can be woven into **cloth**. We wear clothes made of **cloth**.

clothes

This cupboard is full of winter **clothes.** It is full of warm things to wear. Summer **clothes** are light and cool.

cloud

See that dark **cloud** in the sky. A **cloud** is made of tiny water drops. Dark **cloudy** skies often bring heavy rain.

Clowns play in the circus.

clown

The **clown** at the circus makes us laugh. The **clowns** have painted faces and do funny tricks.

club

My cousin plays tennis. He belongs to a tennis **club**. People who share an interest join **clubs.**

clumsy

Someone who is **clumsy** often knocks things over or bumps into things. That **clumsy** dog has upset his drinking bowl.

coach

A **coach** can be a kind of bus. We went on a **coach** trip. A **coach** can also be a trainer or teacher. The **coach** told the team how to play.

coal

Coal is a useful fuel. **Coal** miners dig it from the ground. We burn **coal** to make heat.

coast

Where the land meets the sea is the **coast**. Some **coasts** have high cliffs. A seaport is a **coastal** town.

coat

When we go out we put on a **coat**. Some animals have furry **coats**. Give that door another **coat** of paint.

cobweb

A spider spins a net of silk to catch flies to eat. It spins a **cobweb**.

coconut

The **coconut** palm has a nut called a **coconut**. Inside the brown shell is soft white fruit.

coffee

Coffee is a drink made from the beans of the **coffee** plant. Roasted **coffee** beans are crushed into a powder, and mixed with hot water to drink.

coin

Metal pieces of money are called **coins**. This **coin** is worth ten cents. Ten of these **coins** equal one dollar.

cold

1. On a **cold** day the weather is not hot. The refrigerator keeps food **cold** and fresh.
2. When you catch a **cold**, you sneeze and have a headache.

collar

A **collar** is the band that goes around the neck. A shirt has a collar. My dog's **collar** has his name on it.

collect

Collect your toys. Bring them together so that we can see them. Some people enjoy **collecting** stamps. This is a **collection** of foreign coins.

color

Red is a **color**. So is blue. Flowers are many different **colors**.

come

To **come** means to move toward or to reach. **Come** indoors now, it's dinner time. Sam **came** to visit me in the hospital. Are you **coming** to the shops? There was a lot of **coming** and going at the party.

comic

A **comic** is a paper book with funny stories and drawings inside. Things that are **comic** make us laugh. The clown fell into the water. He looked very **comical**.

computer

A **computer** is an electronic brain. It can do calculations and store information. The travel agent used a computer to book our vacation.

concert

A **concert** is a musical show. The band gave a **concert** in the park.

cook

The **cook** prepares food in the kitchen. This soup is **cooked**. It is ready to eat.

copy

A **copy** of a thing looks exactly like it. Would you like this picture **copied**? Put it on the **photocopier**. You can have two **copies**.

corner

Two straight lines meet at a **corner**. Turn the **corner** and there is our house. I planted a tree in the **corner** of the garden.

correct

Please **correct** this answer. You have gotten it wrong.

costume

We put on Halloween **costumes**. I was dressed up as a fairy. My brother wore a monkey **costume**.

count

Let's **count** the number of cows in the field. Add them up! How many have you **counted**?

country

1. We live in a **country** called France. There are many **countries** in the world.
2. Outside the cities and towns is the **country**. In the country, we can walk in green fields.

couple

A **couple** means two of the same thing. I have a **couple** of coins.

cow

A **cow** is a female member of the cattle family. **Cows** give us milk to drink. Female whales, seals, and elephants are also called **cows**.

cowboy

The **cowboy** rode out to check the cattle. Men who look after herds of cattle are called **cowboys**.

crab

A **crab** lives on the seashore. A crab has a hard shell and sharp claws. Some **crabs** can climb trees!

The **crab** is holding up one of his claws.

crack

A narrow opening is a **crack**. We peered into the cave through a **crack** in the rocks. This cup is **cracked**.

cracker

She had a **cracker** and cheese for her lunch. A **cracker** is a thin, crisp wafer or biscuit.

cradle

A **cradle** is a small, low bed for a baby. The baby girl was fast asleep in her **cradle**. The mother **cradled** the baby in her arms.

crane

A **crane** is a machine that can lift heavy objects. The **crane** driver sits high in the sky.

The **crane** lifts a bucket of concrete.

crash

When things bang into each other, they **crash**. The cars **crashed** in the thick fog. We heard the **crash**.

crawl

Caterpillars **crawl**. So do babies. Before a baby learns to walk, it **crawls** on its hands and knees.

cream

1. **Cream** is the rich, fat part of milk. **Cream** puffs are my favorites.
2. When I cut myself, Mom puts antiseptic **cream** on the cut to heal it.

creature

We are all living **creatures**. The soil is full of tiny living **creatures**.

crocodile

A **crocodile** is a reptile. It is an animal with a scaly body, sharp teeth and short legs. **Crocodiles** live in water.

The **crocodile** is swimming toward us. Crocodiles can be very dangerous.

crooked

Things that are not straight are often **crooked**. That line zigzags — it's **crooked**. There was a **crooked** man, goes the nursery rhyme.

cross

1. Two lines drawn like this + and × make a **cross**. The teacher put a **cross** by every wrong answer. We waited before **crossing** the road.
2. My mother was **cross** because I broke a window. She was angry.

crow

A **crow** is a large, black bird. **Crows** have croaky voices.

crowd

A lot of people together is a **crowd**. On sale days, the stores are very **crowded**.

crown

A **crown** is a headband of gold or silver decorated with jewels. Kings and queens are **crowned**.

The queen is wearing her **crown**.

crush

To **crush** something, you press on it hard and break it into pieces. We **crushed** cookies to make crumbs.

crust

The crunchy, outside part of a loaf of bread is the **crust**. I like **crusty** bread.

cub

A **cub** is a baby animal. Baby bears are **cubs** and so are baby tigers.

cube

Dice are **cubes**. A **cube** is a solid shape with six sides all the same size.

cuckoo

The **cuckoo** is a bird that lays its eggs in another bird's nest. The baby **cuckoo** is fed by its new parents.

curl

A twisted spiral shape is a **curl**. My grannie **curls** her hair. My dog's coat is long and **curly**.

curve

When a line bends in one direction, it makes a **curve**. The road **curved** around the mountain.

cycle

I like to ride my bicycle. I like to **cycle**. I enjoy **cycling**.

cymbals

Cymbals are metal plates that are banged together to make a loud, crashing musical sound.

daisy

A **daisy** is a small white flower. **Daisies** grow in grass. You can make a **daisy** chain by linking the stalks together.

Debbie is making a **daisy** chain.

daffodil

A **daffodil** is a tall yellow flower. **Daffodils** grow from bulbs in spring.

damp

Something is **damp** when it is just wet. Matt came in from the rain and hung his **damp** hat to dry.

dangerous

Dangerous things can do you harm. To skate on thin ice is very **dangerous**.

dark

The sky grows **dark** when the sun goes down. **Dark** things have little light. She has **dark** hair.

date

1. A **date** is the sticky fruit of the **date** palm. I could eat a whole box of **dates**.
2. The **date** of Christmas Day is the 25th of December. The **date** is the day, the month, and the year when something happens.

daughter (daw-ter)

Lynn's parents have two girls. They have two **daughters**.

day

Each **day** lasts for 24 hours. It begins at midnight and ends at the next midnight. There are seven **days** in a week. Each **day** has its own name. During the **daytime** it is light outside. **Daytime** is between sunrise and sunset.

dead

Any animal or plant that is not alive is **dead**. The flowers I picked last week are **dead**. The **death** of our cat made us all unhappy.

deaf

People who are **deaf** cannot hear. We can talk to **deaf** people by using signs.

December

December is the last month of the year.

deep

The well goes down a long way. It is very **deep**. A **deep** river flows between the mountains.

deer

A **deer** is an animal that can run swiftly. Male **deer** grow large branching antlers on their heads.

den

Some wild animals live in a home called a **den**. The bear spent the winter asleep in its **den**.

desert

A **desert** is a land where very little rain ever falls. It is so dry in the **desert** that few plants can grow there. Many **deserts** are covered with sand or stones. **Deserts** are often very hot during the day and cold at night.

A **desert** is very dry.

diamond

A **diamond** is a very hard kind of stone. **Diamonds** usually have no color but they are cut to make them sparkle. **Diamond** jewels cost a lot of money.

Diana has a **diamond** ring.

dice

You need a pair of **dice** to play many board games. A **die** is a cube that has different numbers of dots on each of its six sides. You throw **dice** to start the game.

dictionary

This book tells you the meanings of words. It is a **dictionary**. **Dictionaries** show how words are spelled.

die

Plants and animals **die** when they stop living. The vet gave medicine to our sick cat so that it would not **die**. That plant is **dying**, or has it **died**?

different

Something is **different** if it is not the same. I would like a sweater that is **different** from yours. We had chicken for dinner yesterday but today we'll have something **different**.

difficult

Difficult questions are hard to answer, not easy. I tried to knit a scarf but it was too **difficult**.

dig

The gardener uses a shovel to **dig** up the earth. The pirates **dug** holes in the island when they looked for treasure. They were **digging** for weeks.

Dad is **digging** the garden.

dinner

Dinner is the main meal of the day. We eat **dinner** at 6 o'clock. My parents had a **dinner** party. We have **dinner** in the **dining** room.

dinosaur

No **dinosaur** is alive today. All the **dinosaurs** died a long time ago. They were reptiles.

Diplodocus was the longest **dinosaur**.

dirty

Dirty things are not clean. Your hands are covered with **dirt**.

disappear

To **disappear** means to vanish. The rabbit **disappeared** when the magician waved a wand. It was a strange **disappearance**.

discover

What did you **discover** in the attic? Did you find anything? Scientists often make a new **discovery**. Columbus **discovered** America.

discuss

We want to talk to you about our plans. We want to **discuss** them with you. The teacher had a long **discussion** with my father.

dish

A **dish** is a plate or bowl. We piled strawberries on to our **dishes**.

distance

The **distance** between two places is the space between them. The **distance** between the road and the gate is 50 yards.

disturb

I was fast asleep until a knock at the door **disturbed** me and woke me up. When you **disturb** someone you stop them from going on with what they were doing. People may be annoyed if they are **disturbed**.

ditch

A **ditch** is dug to make a narrow channel. Farmers drain water from their fields into **ditches**.

dive

If you **dive** you jump head first into water. The **diver** is **diving** into the pool.

divide

To **divide** means to break up into smaller parts. We **divided** the cake into four pieces. To **divide** 27 by 9, find out how many times 9 will go into it.

do

To **do** something means to carry out an action. Will you **do** your homework? Yes, I am **doing** it now. I **did** the work properly even if you think I **didn't**. We have **done** a lot of work today.

doctor

When Lucy was ill she went to see the **doctor**. A **doctor** makes sick people better.

dog

A **dog** is an animal that barks. Many people have **dogs** as pets. Wolves are a kind of wild **dog**.

The **dog** is digging up the flowers.

doll

A **doll** is a toy model of a real person. Some **dolls** are made to walk and talk. Sally has a rag **doll**.

This **doll** is wearing a dress.

dollar

The money people use in the United States is called the **dollar**. People use **dollars** in Canada, Australia, and New Zealand too.

done

See **do**.

donkey

A **donkey** is an animal like a small horse. **Donkeys** have long ears and when they bray they make a noise like "ee-aw."

door

A **door** opens and closes the way into a room. **Doors** may be wood or glass. He rang the **doorbell**. She stood on the **doorstep** and asked him to come in. Please wipe your feet on the **doormat** in the **doorway**.

dot

A **dot** is a tiny point. Make a **dot** on the page with your pencil point.

double

1. Paul wanted a **double** helping. He asked for twice as much.
2. Have you ever met your **double**? Your **double** looks exactly like you.

doughnut (doe-nut)

A **doughnut** is a fat, round cake. The baker fries a ball of **dough** and covers it in sugar.

down

Going **down** takes you to a lower place. Let's go **down** to the floor below. **Down** is the opposite of up.

downstairs

Stairs go up and down between the floors of buildings. People go **downstairs** to a lower floor. Some of them may want to come back upstairs again.

dozen

A group of 12 makes a **dozen**.

drag

The log was so heavy we had to **drag** it along with a rope. To **drag** means to pull along. We **dragged** the sled up the hill.

dragon

There is a **dragon** in many old tales. A **dragon** is a make-believe monster with a scaly skin. **Dragons** were supposed to breathe fire through their noses.

The dreadful **dragon** drips and dribbles.

dragonfly

A **dragonfly** is a flying insect with two pairs of bright wings.

drain

A **drainpipe** takes dirty water away. Pour this bucket of dirty water down the **drain**.

draw

1. I **draw** pictures with my crayons. Would you like to see a **drawing** of my dad?
2. The game ended in a **draw**. Nobody won.

drawer

A **drawer** is a tray in which things are kept. Desks have **drawers** which slide in and out. You will find the knives in the **drawer**.

dream

Do you **dream** while you are alseep at night? What did you do in your **dream**? In my **dream** I flew to the moon on an orange with wings. I **dreamt** I was a toadstool. A bad **dream** is called a nightmare. Jack was lost in a **daydream** and he didn't hear the question.

dress

You **dress** when you put on your clothes. Tim got **dressed** after swimming. A **dress** is clothing worn by girls and women. This **dress** has a long skirt and a round neck.

drift

I want to **drift** down the river in a boat. To **drift** means to be carried along. We watched the leaves **drifting** under the bridge. When the wind blows dry snow it piles up into heaps called **drifts**.

drill

A tool that makes holes is a **drill**. The carpenter **drilled** four holes in the wood.

drink

When you feel thirsty you swallow liquid and drink. This **drink** is cold. Jeff **drank** all his medicine. He felt better when he had **drunk** it. Have you been **drinking** my orange juice?

Dave **drinks** a glass of water.

drip

A **drip** is a **drop** that falls. **Drops** of rain **dripped** off the roof. Ink is **dripping** from my pen.

drive

Can you **drive** a car? Can you make it go along the road? The **driver drove** us to the station. The dog was **driving** sheep into a field. The car was **driven** up the driveway to the house.

drop

Don't **drop** the glass. Don't let it fall. He **dropped** the glass and it broke.

drown

People **drown** if they take water into their lungs instead of air. If their lungs fill with water they may die. The man saved his friend from **drowning**.

drum

You beat on a **drum** to make it sound. A **drum** is a thin skin stretched over an empty box. **Drums** are musical instruments.

Danny is a drummer. He plays the **drums**.

dry

If something is **dry** there is no water in it. **Dry** things are not wet. The hairdresser **dried** my hair. The wash is **drying** on the line. Put your wet coat to **dry** near the heater. It will be much **drier** soon. Has the paint **dried** yet?

duck

A **duck** is a bird that lives near water. We went to see the **ducks** swimming on the pond. **Ducks** have skin between their toes to help them swim.

The dirty **duck** dances in the mud.

dull

Dull things are not shiny. Your badge is **dull** and needs a polish. **Dull** also means boring. What a **dull** day. It is raining and there is nothing to do.

during

During means the time while something lasts. The film was so boring that I slept **during** most of it. **During** the show a magician did a trick. **During** also means at some time in.

dust

Dust is tiny specks of dry dirt that fly around in the air. Wipe the **dusty** shelves with a **duster**. I dusted my bedroom yesterday.

dwarf

A **dwarf** is a small person, animal or plant. **Dwarfs** do not grow to full size. We read about Snow White and the Seven **Dwarfs**.

each

Sam, Sarah, and I went to the game. **Each** one of us had a ticket.

eagle

The **eagle** is a large bird of prey. **Eagles** fly high in the sky. They swoop down to catch small animals to eat.

The **eagle** has good eyesight. Its nest is called an eyrie.

ear

We hear sounds with our **ears**.

early

I was **early** for school. I got there before my friends. I woke **early** in the morning. **Early** also means at the beginning of the day.

earring

My sister wears **earrings** on her ears. She likes big, shiny **earrings**.

earth

1. We live on a planet. We call it the **earth**. It travels through space.
2. I dug the **earth** in my garden. Soil is another word for **earth**. I planted seeds in the **earth**.

We all live on planet **earth**.

east

In the morning the sun rises in the **east**. **East** is one of the four directions on a compass or map: north, south, **east**, and west.

Easter

Easter is a springtime holiday. Christian people celebrate **Easter** in memory of the day Jesus Christ rose from the dead. At **Easter** we give presents of **Easter** eggs.

Emma has an exciting **Easter** egg.

easy

Things that are not difficult are **easy**. This problem is simple. I can do it **easily**.

eat

We need to **eat** because our bodies need energy. We get energy from **eating** food. The rabbit **ate** a carrot. Have you **eaten** your vegetables? Can you **eat** any more?

echo

When a sound bounces off high walls it makes an **echo**. I called my name in the cave. The sound **echoed** back again and again.

edge

The **edge** is the end or side of something. Don't go near the **edge** of the cliff. Glue the **edges** together.

egg

All baby animals begin as **eggs**. Birds lay **eggs**. Inside the **egg** is a baby bird.

I like to eat a boiled **egg** for my breakfast

eight (8)

Eight is a number. It is my **eighth** birthday. I am **eight** years old. Spiders have **eight** legs.

either

Choose which color jeans to wear. You can wear **either** the blue ones or the red ones. **Either** and or go together.

elastic

Something that is **elastic** will stretch. A rubber band is **elastic**.

elbow

Halfway up your arm is your **elbow**. It is where your arm bends. My sweater has a hole in the **elbow**.

electricity

Electricity gives us power to make light and move machines. **Electricity** flows along wires. Do you use an **electric** toothbrush?

elephant

The **elephant** is the largest land animal. **Elephants** have trunks and tusks.

An enormous **elephant**

elevator

An **elevator** is a machine that carries people up and down inside a tall building. Let's take the **elevator** to the top floor.

empty

The box is **empty**. There is nothing in it. The opposite of **empty** is full. He **emptied** his money box. No money was left inside.

end

The **end** comes at the finish. We waited for the **end** of the story.

engine

An **engine** is a machine. It uses energy to do work for us. The plane had a powerful jet **engine**. The car **engine** was repaired at the garage. An **engineer** builds **engines**, roads, and bridges.

enjoy

I like dancing. I **enjoy** going to ballet lessons. The dancing is **enjoyable**. Did you **enjoy** your meal?

enormous

An **enormous** thing is very big. We saw a whale. It was **enormous**.

enough

I do not want any more cake. I am full. I have had **enough**. When you have **enough** you have as much as you want.

enter

To **enter** means to come in. We went in through the door marked "**Enter**." It was the **entrance**.

envelope

A letter goes inside an **envelope**. I wrote the address on the **envelope**. I used one of Dad's brown paper **envelopes**.

The **envelope** is open.

equal

Equal means of the same value. 10 is **equal** to 2×5. $2 \times 5 =$ (**equals**) 10.

escalator

An **escalator** is a moving staircase. Hold the rail while riding on the **escalator**!

Elizabeth is on an **escalator**.

40

escape

The hamster tried to **escape** from the cage. It chewed a hole. I saw it **ecaping** and caught it before it could run away.

Eskimo

Eskimos are people who live in the Arctic. They wear warm clothes to keep out the cold.

even

1. **Even** numbers can be divided equally by 2. 2, 4, 6, and 8 are **even** numbers. 1, 3, 5, and 7 are odd numbers.
2. **Even** also means equal. We shared the cakes **evenly**. I had two and Tom had two.

evening

When the sun sets, afternoon has become **evening**. It gets dark during the **evening**.

event

An **event** is when something happens. We took part in three **events** at the sports day.

ever

Ever can mean at any time. Have you **ever** been to Disneyland? **Ever** also means always. They all lived happily **ever** after.

every

Every week that passes my birthday comes nearer. **Every** means each one.

evil

Evil means bad or wicked. The **evil** witch cast a bad spell on Snow White.

exercise

Exercise can mean practice or keeping fit. He goes running for **exercise**. My dog needs lots of **exercise**. This is an **exercise** book. I am doing piano **exercises**.

exit

Exit means the way out. We went through the door marked "**Exit**" to get out of the movie theater.

explain

I can **explain** how to do this experiment. I can tell you the way. Listen carefully while I **explain**.

explode

When something **explodes**, it blows up. An **exploding** bomb makes a loud noise. The bomb is full of **explosives**. It makes an **explosion**.

explore

Let's **explore** the camp site. Let's look all around. We have never been here before. People who **explore** are called **explorers**.

eye

You have one right **eye** and one left **cyc**. Do you have good **eyesight**? The hair growing over your **eye** is an **eyebrow**. Stiff hairs called **eyelashes** help keep dust out of the eye. Your **eyelids** close over your **eyes** when you blink or go to sleep.

face

Your **face** is at the front of your head. Eyes, mouth, nose, chin, cheeks, forehead are all parts of your face. Let's all make funny **faces**!

fact

A **fact** is something that is true. It is a **fact** that China has more people than any other country in the world.

factory

We work in a factory. We make radios. It is a radio **factory**. There are lots of different **factories**.

This **factory** makes fireplaces.

fair

1. **Fair** is a light color. He has **fair** hair.
2. **Fair** also mean to act in a way that is right. That's not **fair**! You cheated! Play the game **fairly**.

fairy

Do you believe in **fairies**? A **fairy** is a tiny make-believe creature. We read about them in **fairy** stories.

fall

1. Take care that you don't **fall** on the ice. When something **falls**, it drops.
2. The **fall** is another name for the autumn. It comes after summer and before winter.

false

When something is **false** it is not true or real. She is wearing **false** eyelashes.

family

In my **family** there is Mom and Dad and my sisters and brothers. Lots of other **families** live in our apartment building. My aunts, uncles, and cousins are also members of the **family**.

far

Far means a long way away. When my cat ran away, we searched **far** and wide for it.

farm

On a **farm**, there are fields of crops, and **farm** animals. **Farming** produces our food. **Farmers** do this job.

fast

A greyhound runs quickly, it runs **fast**. I can run **faster** than you. I won the race.

fat

A hippopotamus looks **fat**. Some **fat** people eat too much. They put on weight. **Fat** is the opposite of thin.

father

A **father** is a male parent. Your **father** and mother are your parents. All the **fathers** entered the parents' race.

favorite

My **favorite** food is salad. I like it better than anything else. It is my **favorite**.

feather

Only birds have **feathers**. A bird's wing has long **feathers**. **Feathers** make a soft filling for pillows.

Five **feathers**

February

February is the second month of the year. On Valentine's Day, 14th **February**, people send each other Valentine cards.

feed

To **feed** means to give food to. The monkeys were **fed** with fruit.

feet

Your shoe goes on your foot. You have two **feet**.

female

A girl or a woman is **female**. Animals and plants can be either male or **female**.

fence

A **fence** keeps things in. A **fence** is made of wood or wire. He climbed the **fence** to get into the park.

A **fence** goes around our garden.

fetch

Fetch means to bring. The dog **fetched** the ball. Go and **fetch** your bag from the car.

field

A **field** is piece of land where grass or crops grow. We worked in the **hayfield**.

fierce

The big dog looked **fierce**. It growled and barked. We were frightened.

fight

The children got angry and had a **fight**. When people **fight**, they attack each other. Later, they are sorry that they **fought**.

Fiona and Frank are **fighting** fiercely.

figure

Figures are signs for numbers. Can you write the **figures** 3 and 8?

fill

Fill the bag with apples. To **fill** means to take up all the space inside something. We **filled** the bag. It was **full** of apples.

film

Sometimes we watch **films** on television. We also put **film** in a camera to take photographs.

fin

The shark swam through the water with its **fin** showing. Fish have bony **fins** to help them steer under water.

find

Did you **find** your lost sock? We did not know where it was. Then we **found** it under the bed. **Finding** it was a bit of luck.

fine

Fine means very good or excellent. As the weather was **fine** we decided to go on a picnic. The teacher had a fine speaking voice.

finger

I point with my **finger**. Do you like long **fingernails**? Humans have five **fingers** on each hand.

finish

To **finish** means to come to the end. When you **finish** your homework, you can watch television. Have you **finished** it all?

fir

A **fir** is a kind of tree that never loses all its leaves. There are forests of **fir** trees in some countries.

fire

Burning wood makes a **fire**. We heard the siren and saw the **fire engine** pass by.

The **fire engine** rushes to the fire.

fire engine

When a building catches fire, the **fire engine** races to the scene. See the firefighters with their hoses! This **fire engine** has a long ladder.

first

First means the beginning. January is the **first** month of the year. I won the race. I came in **first**.

fish

A **fish** is an animal that lives in water. **Fish** have scales and fins. Do you like **fish** sticks?

fist

Close your hand tightly into a ball. This is a **fist**.

fit

1. To be **fit** is to be well and healthy. Plenty of exercise helps us keep **fit**.
2. If something **fits**, it is the right size or shape. This coat is a good **fit**.

five (5)

Five is a number. You have **five** toes on each foot.

flag

Each country has its own **flag**. Can you see the flag fluttering in the breeze? The **flag** is on a **flagpole**.

flake

A **flake** is a small, light bit of something. We eat **cornflakes**. **Snowflakes** are lovely.

flame

We often see a **flame** when a thing burns. Be careful of the **flames** from the fire!

flap

1. A **flap** is a cover or lid. Lift the **flap** of this envelope. Is there a letter inside?
2. **Flap** can also mean to beat. The bird **flapped** its wings as it flew into the tree.

flash

We had our photos taken indoors. The **flash** was very bright. **Flash** means to move very fast. The racing cars **flashed** past.

flat

A **flat** surface is smooth and level. Holland is a **flat** country. There are no high mountains in Holland. This **flat** tire has no air left in it at all.

flavor

The **flavor** of food is how it tastes. There are lots of different **flavors** of ice cream.

float

To **float** means to be held up in the water. A boat **floats** on the sea.

floor

We walk on the **floor** of a room. We have a green carpet on the **floor**. Underneath are **floorboards**. The kitchen **floor** has tiles on it.

flour

The seeds or grains of wheat are crushed into powdery **flour**. With **flour** we make bread and pastry.

flower

The petals of a plant make a colorful **flower**. **Flowers** attract insects to plants. Many **flowers** have a lovely smell.

Flowers of different colors.

fly

1. Birds **fly**. So do many insects. So do airplanes. They all have wings for **flying**. An airliner **flies** high up above the clouds. We all **flew** to New York last year.
2. A **fly** is an insect. Some **flies** carry germs and spoil food.

foal

A baby horse is a **foal**. A **foal** can walk soon after it is born. It stays close to its mother.

fog

A thick mist is **fog**. Drops of water hang in the air. Drivers must take extra care when it is foggy.

fold

Fold this sheet of paper in half. Make a crease down the middle. Now you have **folded** it.

follow

Follow means to come behind. Jim's dog **follows** him to school.

food

We eat **food** to live and keep healthy. Milk, vegetables, and meat are all **foods**.

foot

Your **foot** is at the end of your leg. You walk on two **feet**. A dog's **feet** are called paws.

football

Football is an exciting game played by two teams. It is played with a ball called a **football**.

In some countries soccer is called **football**.

footprint

If you walk on muddy ground, your foot makes a mark called a **footprint.** The detectives found a **footprint** in the garden near the house.

forest

Many trees grow in the **forest**. A **forest** has more trees than a wood. **Foresters** look after the trees.

forget

If you cannot remember something, you **forget** it. I keep **forgetting** where I put my books. He **forgot** to go to the meeting today. He had **forgotten** all about it.

fork

We eat with a knife and **fork**. A **fork** has points or prongs to pick up the food.

forward

Forward is the opposite of backward. To go **forward** is to move ahead.

fountain

A **fountain** is a jet of water which rises into the air. In the park there is a drinking **fountain** where we can get a drink when we are thirsty.

four (4)

Four is a number. This chair has **four** legs.

free

1. A person can do what they want and go where they like. A prisoner is not **free**. **Freedom** is precious.
2. **Free** can mean that something does not cost money. We got a **free** poster from the garage.

freeze

Very cold water may **freeze** into ice. In winter, rivers and ponds **freeze** over. We keep **frozen** food in the **freezer**. Without gloves, my hands felt **freezing** cold.

fresh

Fresh things are new. **Fresh** food is not canned, dried, or frozen. We picked a **fresh** lettuce from the garden. This bread is still warm, it must be **fresh**.

Friday

Friday is the sixth day of the week.

friend

I like my **friend** Sally very much. She is my best **friend**. We always play together. That donkey is **friendly**. It lets us stroke it. The opposite of **friendly** is **unfriendly**.

fright

That bang scared me. It gave me a **fright**. Are you **frightened** of the dark? It's not really **frightening**.

frog

A **frog** is an animal that can live on the land and in the water. It lays its eggs in water. Baby **frogs** are called tadpoles. The **frog** jumped into the pond and swam around. **Frogs**, toads, and newts are called amphibians.

The fearless **frog** leaps from flower to flower.

front

The **front** of a thing is the bit that faces forward. The opposite side to the **front** is the back. Turn to the **front**, please. I want to see your face.

frost

It is so cold that there is **frost** on the ground. **Frost** is ice. On a **frosty** winter's morning the ground is frozen hard.

frown

When you feel worried or are thinking hard, you may **frown**. Your face looks wrinkled. Stop **frowning**. It makes you look angry.

fruit

The **fruit** of a plant is the part that grows around the seed. We can eat some **fruits**. But **fruit** that is not ripe may taste sour and give you a stomachache.

A bowl of fresh **fruit**.

full

My locker is **full** of clothes. There is no room in it for any more. It was empty. Now I have **filled** it. It is **full**.

fun

I'm having a good time. I'm having **fun**. **Funny** stories make us laugh.

fur

Some animals have hairy coats of **fur**. This cat has white **fur**. It is **furry**.

furniture

Furniture means such things as beds, tables, and chairs. Your home has **furniture** in it. It is **furnished**.

gallop

A horse **gallops** when it runs as fast as it can. I can **gallop** on my horse.

game

You play a **game** by the rules. Let's play a card **game**.

gap

A **gap** is a space between two things. Can you see through the **gap** in the fence?

garage

We keep our car in the **garage**. At the **garage** we can buy some gasoline.

Geraldine works at the **garage**.

garden

People can grow flowers or vegetables in their **garden**. A **garden** is a piece of land belonging to a house.

gas

A **gas** has no firm shape and is not a liquid. The air we breathe is a mixture of **gases**. We burn a different **gas** to heat our food and homes.

gate

A **gate** is an outside door. Shut the garden **gate** or the dog will run out.

The girl is leaning on the **gate**.

gather

Gather means to collect things and put them together. Tom **gathered** all his toys from the floor.

gentle

Gentle means soft and kind. I rocked the baby **gently**.

get

To **get** means to fetch or collect or receive. Can I **get** a ticket for the train here? I am **getting** a train ticket for you at the same time.

giant

A **giant** is huge. There are **giants** in fairy tales. Jack climbed the beanstalk and met a **giant**. They sell this soap powder in **giant** boxes.

Gerald the **Giant** has great big gumboots.

gift

A **gift** is a present. People may give us **gifts** on our birthday. Shall we buy a **gift** for Mary?

giraffe

A **giraffe** is an African animal. It has a long neck and long legs. **Giraffes** eat leaves.

girl

My parents have two boys and a **girl**. The **girl** is Sally. She is my sister. Sally is the daughter of my parents. She will be a woman like my mother when she grows up.

The **girl** is wearing Granny's glasses.

give

When you hand something to somebody you **give** it to them. Please **give** me a drink. We **gave** our teacher a birthday present. What are you **giving** her? She was **given** a present.

glad

I am **glad** you came to see me. **Glad** means pleased or happy. Are you **glad** too?

glass

Glass is hard and you can see through it. Bottles are often made of **glass**. Your drinks are in the tall **glasses**. Do you wear **glasses**? Where is the looking **glass**? **Glass** breaks easily.

We drink from **glasses** like these.

glove

Gloves keep your hands warm. **Gloves** cover your hand and each finger.

glue

Glue sticks things together. I am **gluing** a wing on my model aircraft. You can join things together with **glue**.

go

You **go** somewhere when you move from one place to another. Let's **go** for a walk in the park. Is the clock still **going?** Is it still moving or working? She has **gone** to work. I **went** to Spain last year.

goal

A **goal** is something you aim for. To be a doctor was her **goal**. The team scored a **goal** when the puck flew into the net. The **goalkeeper** missed it.

goat

A **goat** is an animal related to a sheep. **Goats** can give milk. Some **goats** have horns.

The **goat** gobbles the geraniums.

God

People worship and say prayers to **God**. We can read about **God** in religious books.

gold

Gold is a shiny, yellow metal. It is dug out of the earth and used to make jewelry and coins. **Gold** is costly.

good

Good things are not bad. You are **good** when you behave well. We had a **good** time when we went to camp. The weather is **good** when it is dry and sunny. My idea is **good**, but yours is **better**. Mom's is the **best** of all.

goodbye

People say **goodbye** when they are going away. He said **goodbye** to the teacher and went home.

goggles

People wear **goggles** to protect their eyes. **Goggles** are like big spectacles. The policeman left his motorcycle and took off his **goggles**. Divers wear **goggles** under the sea.

Gary is wearing **goggles**.

goose

A **goose** looks like a big duck. **Geese** can swim. Some **geese** live on farms. A young **goose** is called a gosling.

The **goose** is standing on one foot.

gorilla

A **gorilla** is the biggest sort of ape. **Gorillas** come from Africa.

grab

To **grab** means to snatch. You take hold of something quickly when you **grab**. He **grabbed** hold of my arm and pulled me out of the pool.

grandparent

My **grandparents** are the parents of my mother and father. I call my mother's parents Gran and Grandpa. I call my father's parents Nan and Grandpop. Your grandfather and your grandmother are your **grandparents.**

grass

Grass ia a plant with thin green leaves. It grows in fields and gardens. Tom cuts the **grass** every week with a lawn mower. Some animals eat **grass.**

great

Great things are large or important. A **great** crowd heard the **great** singer.

greedy

Greedy people want more than they need. They do not like to share with anyone else. He was so **greedy**, he ate all the candy.

greenhouse

A **greenhouse** is made of glass. People grow plants that need extra warmth and shelter in a **greenhouse**.

Geraniums and grapes grow in the **greenhouse**.

grocer

The **grocer** sells foods like tea, sugar, butter, and biscuits. These things are called **groceries**.

ground

The **ground** is the earth we stand and walk on.

group

If a few people collect together, they make up a **group**. The class split into **groups** for the music lesson.

grow

As plants and animals **grow**, they get bigger. Those sunflowers are **growing** high. They have **grown** higher than the fence. **Grow** can also mean to become. It **grew** cold as the snow began to fall.

Gretta is **growing** taller.

growl

Dogs **growl** when they are angry. Please stop your dog from **growling** at my cat.

grunt

A **grunt** is a short, deep sound. Pigs **grunt**.

guard

A **guard** is a person who keeps something or someone safe. There are soldiers on **guard** outside Buckingham Palace in London. To **guard** means to protect.

guess

When you **guess** you try to give the right answer without really knowing if you are right or wrong. **Guess** what the cake weighs.

guitar

A **guitar** is a musical instrument with six strings. A **guitarist** plays by touching the strings with his fingers.

gum

1. The pink flesh around your teeth is called your **gum**.
2. **Gum** is also a kind of glue.
3. Chewing **gum** is a rubbery mixture that often has a minty taste. I also like strawberry chewing **gum**.

gun

A **gun** is a weapon that fires bullets. The farmer shoots his **gun** at birds eating his crops.

gym (jim)

Gym is short for **gymnasium. Gymnasts** do exercises called **gymnastics** in a **gym.**

had See **have.**

hair

Hair grows on your skin. All mammals have **hair** on their bodies. Humans have most **hair** on their head.

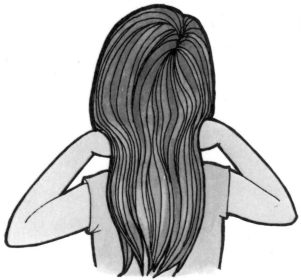

Helen has long **hair.**

50

half (haaf)

If something is cut into two parts that are the same size, each part is a **half.** Two **halves** will make a whole.

Halloween

The date of **Halloween** is 31st October. It is the day before All Saints' Day. We go to **Halloween** parties and bob for apples.

hamburger

A **hamburger** is made of chopped meat. It is flat and round and is cooked by frying. Then it is put inside a **hamburger** bun and eaten like a sandwich.

Harry is eating a huge **hamburger.**

hammer

A **hammer** is a tool for hitting nails into wood. You hold the **hammer** by its long handle and hit the nail with the **hammer** head. The man **hammered** nails into the fence to mend it.

hamster

A **hamster** is a small, furry animal kept as a pet. **Hamsters** store food in their cheeks.

Hamsters make nice pets.

handle

Some things have a **handle** to hold them by. She held the bag by its **handle.** The door **handle** has fallen off.

hang

You hold something up by its top so that it can **hang** free at the bottom. My father is **hanging** a new mirror on the wall. She **hung** her skirt on a hook.

happen

If a thing takes place, it **happens.** What has **happened** at school today?

happy

When people feel cheerful and pleased about something, they are **happy.** We hope you had a **happy** birthday!

hard

Hard things feel firm when you touch them. They are not soft. **Hard** can also mean not easy. This crossword is **hard** to do.

harvest

Farmers gather their crops from the fields at **harvest** time. They bring in the ripe corn and pick fruit and vegetables. In the fall we **harvest** the apples and pears from our garden.

hat

You wear a **hat** on your head to keep it warm and dry. Aunt Jane's **hat** has a feather in it.

Harriet is wearing a horrible **hat**.

hate

If you dislike something very much you may **hate** it. I **hate** washing dishes.

have

You **have** things that you own or hold. Do you **have** a hamster? Yes, and John **has** one too. Before that we **had** a rabbit.

The **helicopter** is taking off.

head

Your **head** is the part of your body above your neck. People's face and hair are part of their **head**.

hear

You **hear** the sounds around you through your ears. Listen, can you **hear** the noise that I am **hearing**.

heart

Your **heart** is the pump that sends blood around your body. Your **heart** is in your chest. After the race my **heart** was beating very fast.

heat

Heat is the warmth that hot things have. We **heated** our milk on the stove.

heavy

Heavy things weigh a lot. This sack of coal is too **heavy** to lift.

helicopter

A **helicopter** is a flying machine. It's rotors spin to keep it in the air. It has no wings.

helmet

People wear hard hats called **helmets** to protect their heads. Motor cyclists must wear a **helmet**.

You should wear a **helmet** to protect your head.

help

You can **help** someone by doing something useful for them. **Help** me clean the windows! Jack **helped** the old lady carry her bags.

51

hen

A **hen** is a female bird. We collect **hen's** eggs to eat for breakfast.

The **hen** is pecking.

here

Here means in this place. **Here** is the book you wanted. Come **here** and show me your work. Can we come **here** again?

hide

When you want to **hide** something, you put it where nobody can see it. **Hide** the present or Jill will see it before her birthday. He **hid** behind the sofa. Where have you **hidden** my candy?

high

Anything **high** is a long way from the ground. Skyscrapers are **high**, and so are mountains. **High** also means the length from top to bottom. This tree is 15 feet **high**.

hill

A **hill** is a place where the ground is higher. We climbed the **hill** to see the whole town below us. The road through the mountains was very **hilly**.

hippopotamus

The **hippopotamus** is a big animal from Africa. It spends a lot of time in water because its body is heavy and it finds it hard to walk on land.

The happy **hippopotamus** hides in the mud.

hit

You strike a ball when you **hit** it. He bumped into the door and **hit** his head.

hold

You **hold** something when you have it in your hands. **Hold** on to the rail as you climb the steps. Eliza **held** Jim's hand.

hole

A **hole** is an opening. I have **holes** in my socks. There are lots of rabbit **holes** in this bank.

home

Home is where you live. I am going **home** to feed my cats.

honey

Honey is a sweet, thick liquid made by bees. I eat golden **honey** on my bread.

hoof

The hard part of a horse's foot is a **hoof**. Pigs and cows also have **hooves**.

hook

A **hook** is a bent piece of metal to catch things on or hang things from. Clothes hang on a **hook**.

hope

When you **hope** for something, you want it to happen. I **hope** we can go riding tomorrow.

horse

A **horse** is an animal used for riding or pulling. **Horses** have tails and manes of long hair. They can gallop fast.

The **horses** hurry home for hay.

hose

A **hose** is a pipe that can be rolled up. It is used to carry water. Firemen sprayed water from the **hose** to put out the fire.

hospital

Sick people go to the **hospital** to be looked at. The doctor took an X ray of my arm at the **hospital**.

hour

An **hour** lasts for sixty minutes. Each day is twenty-four **hours** long.

house

Houses are buildings to live in. My family lives in a **house**. We sometimes help with the **housework**.

how

How is a question that asks the way in which something happens. **How** do you make bread? You can also ask **how** are you? **How** much are they? **How** many?

huge

Huge things are very big. Elephants are **huge** animals.

hump

Camels are animals with **humps** on their backs. A **hump** is a round lump or bump.

hundred

A **hundred** is ten times ten. It is written as 100.

hungry

If you are **hungry** you need something to eat. In winter the **hungry** birds find little food.

hunt

To **hunt** means to look carefully for something. We **hunted** all over the place for Dick's scarf. People also go **hunting** to catch animals. The **hunters** chased after the fox on their horses.

hurry

To **hurry** means to try and do something quickly. If you **hurry** your homework you will make mistakes. She **hurried** to get to the library before it closed.

hurt

Something that **hurts** is painful. Did you **hurt** your arm when you fell off your bicycle?

ice

Frozen water turns to **ice**. We saw skaters at the **ice** rink.

iceberg

An **iceberg** is a large chunk of ice floating in the sea.

The ship sails past an **iceberg**.

ice cream

Ice cream is a cold, sweet food. We made some **ice cream** from cream, sugar, and strawberries.

idea

I had an **idea**. I had a sudden thought. The person who invented the electric light had a good **idea**.

if

When you say "**if**" you mean that something may or may not happen. **If** it stops raining, we can go out to play. **If** Dad gets home early, we can go to the park.

igloo

Eskimos sometimes build a snow house. It is called an **igloo**.

An **igloo** is made of ice.

ill

Tom is not feeling well. He has a cold. He is **ill**.

important

Important means something that matters. This is an **important** meeting. Everyone must come.

in

In describes the place inside. There is a fly **in** my soup.

These **Indians** are different in six ways. Can you see how?

Indian

Someone who was born in India is an **Indian**. The people who lived in America before the Europeans arrived are also called **Indians**.

ink

Ink is a colored liquid. A pen is filled with **ink**.

insect

An **insect** is a small animal with six legs. Bees, ants, and beetles are **insects**.

inside

Inside is the opposite of outside. She is indoors. She came **inside** to get out of the rain.

into

Please enter. Come **into** the room. Get **into** your pajamas.

invite

I want to **invite** everyone to my party. I sent lots of **invitations** asking my friends to come.

iron

1. **Iron** is a metal. **Iron** is dug from the ground. Many tools are made from iron.
2. A hot **iron** presses the creases out of clothes. Do you like **ironing**?

island

A piece of land surrounded by water is an **island**. The West Indies are a group of **islands**. There were trees on the **island**.

jacket

A **jacket** is a short coat. Do you like my riding **jacket**?

jaguar

A **jaguar** is a big wild cat. **Jaguars** have spotted coats. They live in South American forests.

January

January is the first month of the year. The New Year starts on **January** 1st.

jewelry

Necklaces and earrings are **jewelry**. Pretty **jewels** can cost a lot of money.

jet

A hose sends out a **jet** of water. **Jet** engines shoot out **jets** of air.

join

To **join** means to put together. We **joined** hands to make a circle.

joke

A story or saying that makes us laugh is a **joke**. The book was full of funny **jokes**.

juice

The liquid that we squeeze out of fruits is called **juice**. We have orange **juice** for breakfast. This pineapple is very **juicy**.

Janice is drinking orange **juice**.

July

July comes after June and before August. It is the seventh month of the year. We have summer vacations in **July**. **July** is winter in Australia.

jump

To **jump** is to leap in the air. The children **jumped** over each other. Can you see them **jumping**?

Jack is **jumping** over Jane.

June

June comes after May and before July. **June** is the sixth month of the year. Roses flower in **June.**

jungle

A **jungle** is a tangle of trees and bushes. Tigers live in the hot **jungles** of India. Tropical forests are often called **jungles**.

junk

We throw away as **junk** any things we do not want to keep. I found this old tin in a **junk** yard.

kangaroo

A **kangaroo** is a big animal that carries its baby in a pouch on its front. **Kangaroos** live in Australia. They have long tails and strong back legs which they use to jump high in the air.

Kangaroos can jump a long way.

keep

When you hold on to something as your own you **keep** it. May I keep the balloon I found? Are you **keeping** this old bicycle? You also look after things you keep. I **kept** my hamster in a cage.

kettle

You boil water in a **kettle**. Kettles are made of metal and have spouts for pouring. Put the **kettle** on to make tea.

56

key

I use a **key** to open and close the lock on my door. I press the **keys** on a **keyboard** to make a piano, typewriter, or computer work.

kick

When you **kick** something you hit it hard with your foot. He **kicked** the ball past the goal post.

kilt

A **kilt** is a pleated skirt worn by men. Scottish **kilts** are made of a checked cloth called tartan. The Scottish soldiers marched with a band of **kilted** musicians playing the bagpipes and drums.

Kevin is wearing a **kilt**.

kind

This is the **kind** of bicycle I want. What **kind** means the same as what sort or type. **Kind** also means gentle and good to others. She was very **kind** to help me with the shopping.

king

A **king** rules over a **kingdom**. Fewer **kings** rule countries today than years ago. When a **king** is crowned, his wife becomes a queen. Sometimes a queen is crowned and then she rules the country.

The **king** looks at his kingdom.

kitchen

The **kitchen** is the room of a house where food is cooked.

kite

A **kite** is a toy that flies. It is made of paper or cloth stretched over a frame. You hold the **kite** by a long string and let the wind lift it high into the air. Some **kites** have long tails.

knee (nee)

Your **knee** is the joint where your leg bends. When I fell over I hurt my **knees**.

knife (nife)

We use a **knife** for cutting. It has a sharp blade to slice through things. Always pick up **knives** by their handles.

knock (nok)

When you **knock** things you hit or bump into them. Our cat **knocked** the cake off the table. You **knock** at the door when you beat it with your fist. Can you hear someone **knocking** at the door?

knot (not)

A **knot** ties pieces of string, rope, or ribbon together tightly. This wool is all **knotted**.

know (no)

You **know** something if you are sure about it. I **know** your name. I wish I had **known** it was raining. You **know** things that you have seen before. I **knew** the woman in the shop.

ladder

You climb a **ladder** to reach high places. Folding **ladders** are called step-ladders.

You can fold up this **ladder**. It is a step-ladder.

lake

A lake is a large stretch of water with land around it. We sailed on the **lake**. There were high mountains all around the **lake**.

lamb

A **lamb** is a baby sheep. **Lambs** are usually born in the spring.

land

1. The part of the earth that is not covered by water is called **land**. The sailors were glad to reach **land**.
2. Planes **land** at an airport. They come down to the ground. Was it a bumpy **landing**?

language

The people who live in Germany speak the German **language**. These words are written in our **language**.

large

Large means big. That is a **large** dog. It is much **larger** than a mouse.

last

Z is the **last** letter of the alphabet. To be **last** is to come right at the end.

late

If you arrive **late**, you arrive after you are expected. The train is five minutes **late**.

laugh (laf)

People **laugh** at funny things. When you **laugh**, you make a noise that sounds like ha-ha-ha. We **laughed** at the cartoon on TV.

lay

Birds **lay** eggs. A robin **laid** its eggs in the nest.

lazy

Lazy people will not work. He is so **lazy**. He stays in bed all day long watching TV.

leaf

A **leaf** is a green part of a plant. **Leaves** help plants to make food to grow.

These five **leaves** are all different.

learn

When you **learn** something, you find out about it. I am **learning** French. My sister **learned** how to ski.

leave

To **leave** means to go away from. We had to **leave** our class. We **left** when the bell rang. Did you see us **leaving**?

left

Left is the opposite of right. Are you **left**-handed?

leg

Humans have two **legs**. At the end of your **leg** is your foot. Can you hop on one **leg**?

lemon

The **lemon** is a yellow fruit. **Lemon** juice tastes very bitter.

lend

Please **lend** me your book! I only want it for a little while; then you can have it back. She **lent** me the book. I borrowed it.

leopard

A **leopard** is a big, spotted cat. **Leopards** can climb trees. A **leopard** is a fierce hunter.

The lazy **leopard** lies among the leaves.

lesson

We learn a **lesson**. Children have **lessons** in school. Today we had a swimming **lesson**. My teacher took driving **lessons**.

let

To **let** means to allow. **Let** Tony take a turn on your bicycle. He **let** you have his ball.

letter

1. A **letter** is a written message. I wrote a **letter** to my cousin. I put the **letter** in the **letter** box.
2. A **letter** is also a part of the alphabet. A, B, C, and D are **letters**.

library

A **library** is a place where books are kept. We borrowed the books from the **library**. The **librarian** helped us find the ones we wanted.

lie

1. **Lie** down if you are tired. Stretch out on the bed and go to sleep.
The dog is **lying** on the carpet.
2. When people don't tell the truth, they **lie**. Tom said his name was Simon. He was **lying**. He **lied** about his name.

lift

To **lift** means to raise a thing. She **lifted** the heavy box.

light

1. **Light** comes from the sun, the stars, and lamps. Put on the **light**; it's dark in here.
2. **Light** also means not heavy. Feathers are **light**.

lighthouse

A **lighthouse** has a light to warn ships of dangerous rocks at sea. The **lighthouse** is a tall tower where **lightkeepers** work.

The **lighthouse** flashes in the dark.

lightning

Sometimes, we see a flash of **lightning** during a storm. **Lightning** is a giant electric spark. The noise of thunder follows the **lightning**.

like

1. I **like** my friends. I enjoy playing with them. I **like** reading too. I enjoy reading a book.
2. That boy is **like** his brother. They look and act the same. Can you see the **likeness**?

lion

The **lion** is a big, wild cat. Male **lions** have thick hair around their necks called manes. A female **lion** is a **lioness**.

The **lion** loves to roar.

lip

Around your mouth are your **lips**. You have a top **lip** and a bottom **lip**. When you say "oooo" your **lips** make an O shape.

listen (liss-en)

Listen to the music. We can all hear it. We are all **listening**. They **listened** to what the teacher said.

little

Little things are small, not big. Piglets are baby pigs. They are **little**.

live

We **live** in the city. The city is our home. My uncle **lives** in Canada. He once **lived** in Australia.

lock

A door has a **lock**. Turning a key **locks** the door. When the door is **locked** you cannot open it.

look

When we use our eyes, we are **looking** at things. **Look** at the picture. The children **looked** both ways before crossing the road.

lose (looz)

When you **lose** something you cannot find it. He was always **losing** his pen. The strangers were **lost** in the forest.

loud

A **loud** sound makes a lot of noise. I banged the drum **loudly**. Everyone heard the **loud** noise.

machine

We make **machines** to help us do work. **Machines** make most of the things we buy. **Machines** at home help us sew, cook, and clean. We clean carpets with a **machine** that sucks up dust. A refrigerator is a **machine** that keeps food fresh.

magic

A magician may say **magic** spells to make strange things happen. A **magician** makes **magic**.

magnet

A **magnet** is a piece of metal that can pull iron and steel toward it. You can pick up pins with a **magnet**.

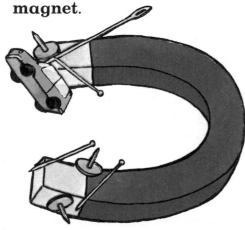

What has the **magnet** picked up?

make

You **make** something that you build or put together. What are you **making** with that wood?

male

Men and boys are **male** humans. **Male** is the opposite of female.

mammal

A **mammal** is an animal that can feed its young with milk from its body. Humans are **mammals** and so are mice and whales.

The mammoth was a **mammal**.

man

A **man** is a male human. When boys grow up they become **men.**

many

Many means a lot. I have **many** toys. How **many** fingers do you have? This means what number.

map

A **map** is a plan of a place. It shows where roads, towns, countries, seas, and mountains are. This **map** shows our way home.

march

To **march** means to step in time to a beat. The soldiers **marched** home to the beat of a drum.

March

March comes after February and before April. It is the third month of the year.

mark

A **mark** is a spot or some kind of written sign. There is a dirty **mark** on your shirt.

marry

When a man and woman become husband and wife, they **marry**. When my sister **marries**, there will be a big wedding. My parents were **married** in a church.

mask

A **mask** is a cover for the face. Hospital doctors may wear **masks** to stop spreading germs.

match

1. We can strike a **match** to light a fire. Do you have a box of **matches**?
2. Does this blue hat **match** the color of my coat? **Match** can mean to sort by size, shape, or color. A game between two teams or people is called a **match**. Sue won the tennis **match**.

You should never play with **matches**.

May

May comes after April and before June. It is the fifth month of the year.

meal

Breakfast, lunch, dinner, and supper are **meals**. Lunch is my favorite **meal** of the day.

measure

We **measure** things to find out how big they are. **Measure** the length of the hall. I **measured** the right amount of medicine into the glass.

meat

Meat is the flesh of an animal used for food. Pork is the **meat** of a pig. Animals that eat **meat** are called "carnivores." Roast beef is my favorite **meat**.

medicine

If you are ill, you take **medicine** to get better. The **medicine** the doctor gave me cured my cold.

meet

When you **meet** people, you come face to face with them. I am **meeting** my mother in the restaurant. Have you **met** my mother?

melon

A **melon** is a large, juicy fruit with a thick skin. If you are thirsty on a hot day, eat some **watermelon**.

Melons are juicy and sweet.

melt

Ice cubes turn to water as they **melt**. Some things **melt** to a liquid when they are heated.

mend

I broke my plate but was able to **mend** it with glue. This broken radio needs **mending**. Who will make it work again?

metal

Things made of **metal** are hard and strong. Iron, steel, and tin are all **metals**.

microscope

A **microscope** makes tiny things look much bigger.

middle

The **middle** of something is the center of it. Divide this pie down the **middle**.

midnight

A day ends at **midnight**. Twelve o'clock at night is **midnight**.

milk

Milk is a white liquid we like to drink. Some animals make **milk** to feed their young. We get our **milk** from cows and goats.

minute

A **minute** lasts for 60 seconds. It will be two o'clock in just three **minutes**. There are 60 **minutes** in an hour.

mirror

A **mirror** is a piece of glass that shows you what you look like.

mistake

Jim put the wrong date on the letter. He made a **mistake**. I'm sorry, I **mistook** you for your brother. No, you are **mistaken**.

mix

Mix the flour with the shortening and sugar. Stir the **mixture** together.

money

Money is the coins and paper notes used to buy things. I keep my **money** in a **moneybox**.

monkey

A **monkey** is an animal that lives in the jungle. **Monkeys** swing through the trees with their long arms, legs, and tails.

The **monkey** is mixing milk with marmalade.

monsoon

The **monsoon** is a wind that brings heavy rain to hot countries in the summer. In winter it blows dry air.

month

There are twelve **months** in a year. The **months** of the year are January, February, March, April, May, June, July, August, September, October, November, and December.

moon

The **moon** revolves around our earth. The **moon** shines in the night sky. A new **moon** is thin, but see the **moonlight** from the round full **moon**.

more

I have **more** badges than Tim. I have a larger number of badges than he has.

morning

Morning is the part of the day before noon. We must get up and go to school in the **morning**.

mosque

A **mosque** is a building where people who are Muslims go to worship.

moth

A **moth** is an insect that looks like a butterfly. **Moths** fly mostly at night.

mother

A **mother** is a woman who has a child. Your **mother** is your female parent.

mountain

A **mountain** is a very high hill. The highest **mountain** in the world is Everest.

The peaks of the **mountains** are covered in snow.

mouse

A **mouse** is a small, furry animal with a long tail and sharp teeth. Some **mice** live in houses. Most **mice** live in woods and fields.

mouth

Your **mouth** is the part of your face that you use to eat and speak. The teeth in your **mouth** bite food, and your tongue tastes it. You open your lips to put food in your **mouth** and to talk.

move

Something **moves** when it goes from one place to another. You are **moving** when you jump or skip or run. Have you **moved** my book?

much

Much means a large amount. You are making too **much** noise.

How much tea is in the **mug**?

mud

Mud is soft, wet earth. There was **mud** from the garden all over our shoes.

multiply

When you **multiply**, you make a number bigger. Four **multiplied** by two equals eight.

muscle

A **muscle** is a part of your body that helps you to move. You need your arm **muscles** to lift things. The weightlifter had huge **muscles**.

music

Sounds from a singing voice or a **musical** instrument make **music**. I am learning to play the recorder in my **music** lessons.

nail

1. A **nail** is a small piece of pointed metal that is used to join pieces of wood together. **Nails** are hit into wood with a hammer.
2. The hard parts on the ends of your fingers and toes are **nails**.

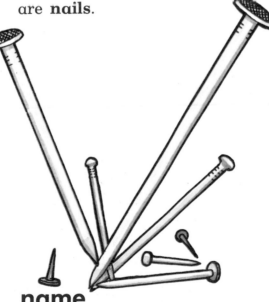

name

Every person and every thing has a **name**. My **name** is John Brown. My pet fish is **named** Flipper.

nature

Nature is everything in the world not made by people. Mountains, rivers, plants, and animals are all parts of **nature**.

naughty (naw-tee)

If you are **naughty** you do not behave well. Were you **naughty** today?

near

A thing that is **near** is not far away. The train drew **nearer** the station.

neck

Your **neck** is the part of your body between your head and your shoulders. She wore a warm scarf around her **neck**.

She is wearing a **necklace**.

need

If you **need** something you must have it. I **need** something to drink. Jenny was so tired that she **needed** a rest. Do you **need** any money?

neighbor

People who live near you are your **neighbors**. The ball landed in our **neighbor's** garden.

nephew

The son of your brother or sister is your **nephew**.

nest

A bird makes a **nest** to lay its eggs in. Birds weave their **nests** from twigs, leaves, mud, and straw.

The chicks are in their **nest**.

net

A **net** is made of string knotted loosely into a pattern of holes. We caught fish in our **net** as we dragged it through the water.

never

Never means not at any time. I **never** eat bananas. We are **never** late for school.

new

New things have just been made or bought. We bought a **new** carpet when the old one wore into holes.

newspaper

A **newspaper** is printed words and pictures on paper sheets. It tells you what is happening in the world.

niece

My aunts and uncles call me their **niece**. They are the brothers and sisters of my parents. I am the daughter of my parents. My sisters are also the **nieces** of my uncles and aunts.

night

Night lasts from sunset to sunrise. It is dark. People go to bed at **night**.

nine (9)

Nine is the number that comes before ten.

nobody

Nobody means the same as no person or no-one. I heard a knock but **nobody** was there.

noise

A **noise** is a sound that you hear. Children shouting in the playground made a loud **noise**.

noon

Noon is the middle of the day. It is midday at 12 o'clock **noon**.

north

North is the direction that is the opposite of south. The wind blew from the **north**.

nose

The **nose** is the part of your face that you use to breathe and to smell. Most animals have **noses**.

nothing

If you do not have anything, you have **nothing**. An empty room has **nothing** inside it.

November

November is the month after October and before December. It is the eleventh month of the year.

now

Something that happens **now** is happening at this moment. Will you go for a walk **now** or later?

number

A **number** is a word or figure that tells you how many. 3, 4, and 5 are **numbers**. I have a **number** of pens. Think of a large **number** and we will try to guess it. The pages of this book are **numbered**.

nut

A **nut** is a fruit or seed inside a hard shell. We crack **walnuts** open with **nutcrackers**.

oak

The **oak** is a tree. **Oaks** live for hundreds of years. The seeds of the **oak** tree are called acorns.

ocean

Oceans are huge seas. The Pacific **Ocean** is the largest **ocean** in the world. The Atlantic and Indian **Oceans** are smaller.

o'clock

When you look at the clock to tell the time, do you use the word **o'clock**? We got up at seven **o'clock**.

October

October is the tenth month of the year.

odd

1. Any number that cannot be divided by two is an **odd** number. 3, 5, 7, 9, and 11 are **odd** numbers.
2. Odd means strange or unusual. The engine is making an **odd** noise.

off

Off means the opposite of on. Take **off** your coat. Switch **off** the television.

offer

If you **offer**, you say you will do something. We **offered** to pay for the window we broke.

often

Often means over and over again. We go to the park every week. We **often** go there.

oil

Oil is a thick liquid found in rocks under the ground. A hole dug to find **oil** is an **oil** well. We burn **oil** in machines. Plastics are made from **oil**. We also get vegetable **oil** from plants.

one (1)

If a thing is on its own, there is just **one** of it. There is **one** bird on the branch. I was the only **one** wearing pink socks.

onion

An **onion** is a round vegetable. Peeling **onions** makes me cry.

Onions grow under the ground.

only

Mary was the **only** girl on the team. All the others were boys. **Only** means just one of a kind.

open

You can walk through an **open** door. **Open** is the opposite of closed. He **opened** the door. Do you want it left **open**?

orange

An **orange** is a juicy fruit. **Orange** is also a color. **Orange** things are the same color as an **orange.**

An **orange** quenches your thirst.

orchard

An **orchard** is a place where fruit trees grow. Apples are grown in an **orchard**.

organ

The **organ** is a musical instrument. There are pipe organs and electronic **organs**. Someone who plays the **organ** is an **organist**.

ostrich

The **ostrich** is the biggest of all birds. **Ostriches** cannot fly.

other

This is my room. Yours is the **other** room. Keep this secret to yourself. Don't tell the **others**.

out

Out is the opposite of in. Don't play indoors. Go **out** in the garden. I looked **out** of the window. I went to see my friend, but she was **out**. Let the mouse **out** of its cage!

outside

Outside means not inside. Wear your coat when you go **outside** the house. It's cold **outside**.

oval

Oval means shaped like an egg. The running track was **oval** in shape.

oven

We bake pies in an **oven**. The **oven** is in the stove.

over

Over means above. **Over** is the opposite of under. Hold the umbrella **over** your head or you will get wet. The bird flew **over** the fence.

owl

An **owl** is a bird that hunts at night. **Owls** can see well in the dark. Did you hear the **owl** hoot?

The **owl** hoots at night.

pack

To **pack** is to put things into a container. We **packed** our clothes into a bag. The bus is **packed**. It is full of people.

66

paddle

1. A **paddle** is a small oar. We **paddled** the canoe across the lake.
2. To **paddle** also means to walk in shallow water. Ben **paddled** in the stream.

paddock

A **paddock** is a field with a fence round it. My pony lives in the **paddock**.

paint

Paint is a colored liquid. When we **paint** we put colors on paper or objects. The **painters** came to our house. They **painted** it green.

pair

Two things that go together are a **pair**. I wear a **pair** of socks and a **pair** of shoes.

palace

Kings and queens live in fine houses called **palaces**. We went to see the **palace**.

This is a pretty pink **palace**.

pan

A **pan** is a flat dish used for cooking food. We washed up the pots and **pans**.

panda

A giant **panda** is an animal that lives in China. **Pandas** have black and white fur and eat bamboo shoots.

The **panda** pats the pine cone.

paper

Books and newspapers are printed on **paper**. We write on **paper**. **Paper** is made from trees. Do you like the **wallpaper** in my bedroom.

parachute

Wearing a **parachute** you can jump out of a plane, and float down gently to earth. You will be a **parachutist**!

The **parachutist** has jumped out of an airplane.

parade

We all watched the **parade** go past. There was a band in the **parade** led by a drum major.

parent

A **parent** is a mother or father. Are those people in the photo your **parents**?

park

1. A **park** is a large area of grass and trees. People go to the **park** on warm, sunny days.
2. To **park** a car means to stop at the roadside or in a **parking** lot. We **parked** the car close to the beach.

parrot

A **parrot** is a brightly colored bird. Some **parrots** talk. The **parrot** copies its owner's voice. My **parrot** says "Pretty Polly."

A **parrot** perched on a plant pot.

part

A **part** is a piece of something. This machine is broken. It needs a new **part**. Your arm is **part** of your body. I saved **part** of my pocket money.

party

A **party** is a group of people. A **party** of children went to the zoo. All my friends came to my birthday **party**.

pass

To **pass** means to go ahead of. The fast car **passed** us.

past

Something that happened yesterday, or much longer ago, happened in the **past**.

path

We walked on a **path**. A **path** is a walkway. There are flowers on either side of the **path**. We followed **paths** through the woods.

paw

The foot of an animal with claws is its **paw.** We saw the **paw** marks of a fox in the mud by the pond.

pay

You **pay** money when you buy something. What did she **pay** for that dress? She **paid** too much for it.

pea

A **pea** is a climbing plant. Round **peas** are the seeds of the **pea** plant.

There are lots of **peas** in a pea-pod.

peace

Peace means stillness. It was quiet and **peaceful**. The war ended. There was no more fighting. There was **peace**.

peach

A **peach** is a fruit with fuzzy skin, that grows on trees in warm countries.

pear

A **pear** is a fruit with a wide bottom and narrow top. **Pears** grow on **pear** trees.

pedal

Pedal the bicycle to make the wheels turn around. Put your feet on the **pedals**.

peel

You **peel** a fruit or vegetable to take off its skin.

pen

A **pen** is used to write. **Pens** are filled with ink. I have a blue **pen**.

penguin

A **penguin** is a bird. **Penguins** swim in the sea to catch fish. **Penguins** cannot fly.

Penguins like the cold.

people

All human beings are **people**. The world is full of **people**.

person

A single human being is a **person**. You are a **person**. I like that **person**. She is one of my favorite **people**.

Who is in the **photograph**?

photograph (foe-toe-graff)

A camera can take a **photograph**. She is a professional **photographer**. Look at my **photograph** album.

piano

A **piano** is a musical instrument. The **piano** keys cause hammers to hit the strings and make music.

pick

1. To **pick** up something is to lift it. I **picked** up my shoes.
2. **Pick** can also mean choose. I **picked** the black puppy, not the white one.

The **picnic** looks delicious.

picnic

A **picnic** is a meal you eat outdoors. We took a **picnic** lunch to the beach. We took food and drink with us.

picture

A **picture** is a drawing or painting. Did you draw this **picture**? Some of the **pictures** in this book make me laugh!

pie

A **pie** is made with pastry. Pastry is made of flour and butter. The farmer ate pumpkin **pie**. Who would like some apple **pie**?

piece

A **piece** of something is a part of it. Would you like a **piece** of cake? When you finish a jigsaw all the **pieces** fit together.

pig

A **pig** is a farm animal. The meat from **pigs** is called pork. A baby **pig** is a **piglet**.

pile

A **pile** means a heap. We raked the leaves into a **pile**. We **piled** them high.

pill

A **pill** can make a sick person better. Powdered medicines can be made into **pills**. **Pills** must be kept in a safe place.

pilot

A **pilot** flies an airplane. The **pilot** took the controls for the landing.

pineapple

A **pineapple** is a fruit that grows in warm countries. **Pineapples** are prickly. But inside the **pineapple** is sweet and juicy.

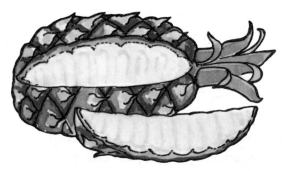

place

1. To **place** a cup on the table means to put it there. **Place** the jug on the shelf.
2. Let's find a **place** where we can sit down. **Place** can mean an area or position. This my **place**. Go and sit somewhere else.

planet

A **planet** is a world spinning through space. Earth is a **planet**. Nine **planets** spin around our sun.

plant

A **plant** is a living thing. Unlike animals, **plants** cannot move. Most **plants** have leaves, roots, and flowers. We **planted** seeds.

play

1. We like to **play** with our friends. We have fun **playing** games and sports.
2. At the theater we saw a **play**. Actors and actresses are sometimes called **players**.

plum

The **plum** is a small, round, dark red or purple fruit. **Plums** grow on **plum** trees.

pocket

A **pocket** is a pouch for putting things in. I lost some money. There was a hole in my **pocket**.

poison

A person who swallows **poison** may become so ill that they die. Some plants and animals have dangerous **poisons**. The rattlesnake is a snake with a **poisonous** bite.

police

Police are the people who make sure everyone obeys the laws of a country. A **policewoman** showed us how to cross the road.

polish

Polish is a kind of wax that you rub on a surface to make it shine. He **polished** his shoes before he went to school.

polite

It is **polite** to say "please" and "thank you."

pond

A **pond** is a very small lake. Water with land all around it is a **pond**. Ducks swim on the **pond** in the park.

pony

A **pony** is a small horse. The children learned to ride on friendly **ponies**.

pool

A **pool** can be a pond. A **pool** can also be a place where we go swimming.

poor

People who have little money are **poor**. **Poor** people are not rich.

popular

Someone who is liked by everyone is **popular**. John is the most **popular** boy at our school.

population

Population is the number of people living in a place. What is the **population** of Los Angeles?

pot

A **pot** is a deep dish used for cooking. **Pots** normally have handles.

potato

The **potatoes** we eat grow on the roots of the **potato** plant.

pour

Pour some water from the pitcher. She **poured** cream over her pie. When something is **poured**, it is tipped out of its container.

pretty

We like to see **pretty** things. I made a **pretty** pattern.

price

How much money you pay to buy something is its **price**. Can you tell me the **price** of that book?

print

To **print** means to press marks or patterns with ink on to paper or fabric. The words and pictures in this book are **printed**. If you step into wet cement, your foot makes a **footprint**.

prize

I won the **prize** for the best drawing.

pudding

A **pudding** is a sweet food. Rice **pudding** is soft and milky.

puddle

After the rain, there were lots of **puddles** in the street. A **puddle** is made when water cannot drain away.

pull

Pull means to get hold of something and move it toward you or in the same direction as you. The tractor **pulled** the plow.

puppet

A **puppet** is a doll you can work to make it move. Some **puppets** are worked by pulling strings. You wear a hand **puppet** on your hand.

puppy

A **puppy** is a baby dog. A mother dog has a litter of **puppies**. A **puppy** is also called a pup.

purse

A **purse** is a small bag that closes tightly. People carry their money and small belongings in a **purse**.

push

To **push** mean to move something away from you. **Push** the door so we can go out.

put

Put your clothes away. Lay them in the drawer. Did you **put** your name on the list?

puzzle

A **puzzle** is a problem that is difficult to solve. Sometimes a **puzzle** has a trick answer. Wendy put a piece in the jigsaw **puzzle**.

quack

I can hear a duck! **Quack, quack** it says.

quarrel

When you argue and get angry with a person, you **quarrel**. The boys **quarreled** over who won the game.

quarter

A **quarter** is a fourth part. If you divide a pie into **quarters**, you cut it into four pieces.

queen

A female monarch or ruler is called a **queen**. **Queen** Mary was the wife of King William.

The **queen** holds a quacking duck.

question

'What is your name?' I ask a **question**. 'Tom,' you reply. You answered my **question**.

quick

Quickly means fast, in a short time. The horse is **quick**. It gallops **quickly**.

quiet

When it is **quiet**, there is hardly any noise. Be **quiet** or you'll wake the baby.

quiz

In a **quiz** someone asks questions and other people give the answers.

rabbit

A **rabbit** is a small furry animal. **Rabbits** have long ears and hop when they run.

The **rabbit** rushes to its burrow.

race

In a **race**, people try to see which of them is fastest. The runners **raced** around the track. It was exciting watching the **racing** cars.

radio

A **radio** picks up programs from a **radio** station. I heard the news on my car **radio.**

raffle

Buy a **raffle** ticket! If yours has the lucky numbers, you win a prize.

railroad

A train runs on long strips of metal called **rails**—a **railroad**. The train is pulled by a **railroad** locomotive.

rain

Rain is the water that falls from clouds in the sky. A **rainbow** is a band of color made by sunlight bouncing off **raindrops**.

Rain is falling in a puddle.

raise

To **raise** something means to lift it up. I **raised** my arms above my head.

read

When you **read** a book you look at the words in the book and understand what they mean. Do you like **reading**?

ready

We are **ready**. We are able to begin. We have all we need. We were **ready** for breakfast. We got **ready** to go to the party.

real

Something you can believe is **real**. This **really** happened. It is true.

record

1. A **record** is a disc you play when you want to listen to music. 2. A **record** is also the best anyone can do. He set a world **record** for the long jump.
3. A **record** can be a true story. The travelers kept a **record** of their journey in notebooks.

red

Red is a bright color. **Red** can mean danger. Watch out for the **red** stop light!

remember

We **remember** things we don't forget. To **remember** something is to keep it in your mind. I **remembered** Jane's birthday.

reply

A **reply** is an answer. Please **reply** to this invitation. He **replied** that he would not be able to come to the party.

rhinoceros

Rhino is short for **rhinoceros**. **Rhinos** live in Africa and Asia. Can you see the **rhino's** horns?

rhyme

Words that **rhyme** sound the same. "Bee" **rhymes** with "sea". Some poems have **rhymes**.

rib

A **rib** is a bone. Can you feel the **ribs** in your chest? The **rib** bones form a kind of cage.

ribbon

A **ribbon** is a narrow piece of material. Some people tie their hair back with **ribbons**.

Rita has red **ribbons** in her hair.

rich

1. **Rich** people have a lot of money. That **rich** man is a millionaire.
2. The soil is **rich**. Plants grow well in it.

ride

We can **ride** on animals or machines. Emma **rides** a horse. Tim **rode** his bicycle to school yesterday. Have you ever **ridden** a horse or a bicycle?

Ron is **riding** a pony.

right

1. This answer is **right**. It is correct. Can you show me the **right** way to do this? If something is not **right**, it is wrong.
2. Hold up your **right** hand. **Right** can also mean the opposite of left. Turn **right**, not left, at the crossroads.

ring

1. A **ring** is a circle. You wear a **ring** on your finger.
2. A bell **rings**. The telephone **rang** but nobody answered. Have you **rung** the doorbell?

rise

To **rise** means to move upward. The sun **rises** in the morning. The plane **rose** high in the sky.

river

Water flowing from the hills to the sea is a **river**. **River** water is fresh. Bridges carry roads across **rivers**. The fishermen sat on the **river** bank.

road

A **road** is a highway or street. Cars and trucks travel on **roads**. The Romans built good **roads**. Look both ways before you cross the **road**.

roar

A **roar** is a lound noise. The lion **roared** all night.

rob

To **rob** means to steal or take things that do not belong to you. The **robbers** took money from the bank. They **robbed** the bank.

rock

1. If something **rocks**, it moves gently from side to side. The baby was **rocked** in its cradle.

2. The earth is made of a hard material called **rock**. We picked up **rocks** on the mountain. It was very **rocky**.

rocket

A **rocket** shoots up in the air. Big **rockets** go into outer space.

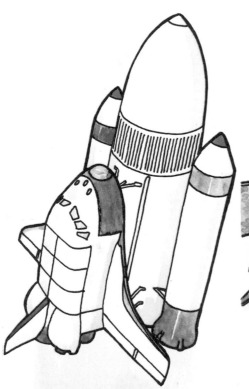

The **rocket** blasts off into the sky.

roll

Roll means to turn over. **Roll** the ball. **Roll** out of bed.

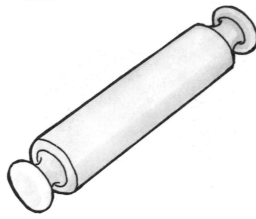

You can roll pastry with a **rolling pin**.

roof

The roof is the top part of a building or vehicle. The **roofs** of houses stop rain and snow from getting in. We had a **roof** rack on top of the car.

root

The **root** of a plant holds it in the ground. With its **roots** a plant takes in food and water.

rope

A **rope** is made from cords twisted together. We slid down the **rope**. The boat was tied to the jetty by a **rope**.

rose

A **rose** is a plant with beautiful flowers. Gardens with **roses** in them smell nice too.

Roses grow on bushes. They have sharp thorns.

round

A **round** shape looks like a circle or a ball. The sun is **round**.

rub

When you **rub** your hands together they feel warm. **Rubbing** a table top with polish makes it shiny.

rule

A **rule** is like a law. Play the game by the **rules**. In the U.S.A. cars drive on the right. That is the **rule**.

run

When we **run**, we are moving as fast as our legs will go. The horse was **running** around the track. My dog is a fast **runner**. She **ran** after a rabbit.

Rosemary is **running** around the rose bush.

sad

When we are unhappy we feel **sad**. Jan felt **sad** when she lost her favorite toy.

sail

The **sail** on a **sailboat** is a large sheet of cloth. The wind hits the **sail** and pushes the boat forward. When we go out in a boat with a **sail**, we are **sailing**. People who go **sailing** are called **sailors**. Peter **sailed** his ship on the pond.

salt

We add **salt** to our food to make it tasty. **Salt** is made up of tiny white crystals.

sand

Sand is made from tiny pieces of rock. I love to dig with my shovel on a **sandy** beach. We made a **sandcastle**.

saw

A **saw** is a tool with sharp teeth for cutting wood and metal. Dad made lots of **sawdust** when he **sawed** the logs.

school (skool)

We go to **school** to learn things. **School** teachers show us how to read and write. We make lots of **schoolfriends**.

scissors (sizz-ers)

Scissors have two sharp metal blades for cutting. The blades are fixed together at the middle. We hold **scissors** in our fingers and move the blades against each other to cut paper and cloth. We cut our nails with **scissors**.

The **scissors** are sharp.

scratch

When you rub an itch, you **scratch** it. When you make a **scratch**, you mark something with a sharp edge. Who **scratched** the table? Our dog is always **scratching**.

screen

Televisions and computers have **screens**. The **screen** shows pictures and words.

screw

A metal **screw** holds two pieces of wood together. A nail is smooth, but a **screw** has a grooved edge to grip the wood. You turn the **screw** into the wood with a **screwdriver**.

sea

The salt water that covers most of the earth is called **sea**. There are lots of fish in the **sea**.

seal

1. A **seal** is an animal that lives in or near the sea. **Seals** have flippers.
2. A **seal** fastens something. This envelope has a sticky **seal**.

season

There are four **seasons** to a year. Spring, summer, fall, and winter are the four **seasons**.

see

You **see** with your eyes. Have you **seen** a blue moon? Yes, I **saw** it last night when I looked out of the window.

seed

Many plants grow from tiny **seeds**. A flower leaves **seeds** behind when it dies. Let's plant **seeds** in the garden.

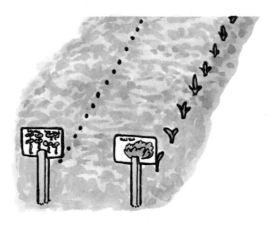

The **seeds** will grow into plants.

sell

People **sell** you things if you pay money for them. The storekeeper **sells** the things that you buy.

September

September comes after August and before October. **September** is the ninth month of the year.

seven (7)

Seven is a number. Each week has **seven** days in it.

shadow

If something stands in the way of a light, it will make a dark **shadow** on the ground. The candle made flickering **shadows** on the wall of the dark room.

My **shadow** is very long.

shake

You **shake** things when you move them quickly up and down or from side to side. The wet dog **shook** water from its coat. I saw the two men **shaking** hands.

shape

Everything we can see has a **shape**. A ring is a round **shape**. The line around the outside of something makes its **shape**.

share

If people give you a part of what they have you **share** it.

sharp

Sharp things have a cutting edge or a point. A **sharp** knife will cut the string.

sheep

A **sheep** is a farm animal. **Sheep** have a thick coat of hair called wool. We make cloth from wool.

It is snowing on the **sheep**.

shell

A **shell** is a hard outside cover. Many animals and fish have **shells** that protect their soft bodies. The snail hides in its **shell** when it is frightened. Eggs and nuts are protected in **shells**. Sea **shells** are the coverings of small sea animals.

shine

Bright things **shine** as they give out light. When the sun is **shining**, my room lights up. My shoes are **shiny**.

ship

A **ship** is a big boat. Some **ships** take people across the ocean.

shirt

A **shirt** is worn on the top half of the body. It can have sleeves and a collar and buttons down the front. I put on my pants first and then my **shirt**.

shop

A **shop** sells things that we buy. We go to different **shops** for our **shopping**. We **shop** for bread at the bakery.

short

Short things are not long. We are **short** of coffee. We do not have enough.

shoulder

Your **shoulder** joins your arm to the rest of your body. Grandma put a shawl over her **shoulders.**

shout

A loud call is a shout. The boy **shouted** across the street to his friend.

show

To **show** means to point out something or let somebody see it. Can you **show** me the bus stop? **Show** me the shoes you bought yesterday.

shut

Shut means the same as close. You **shut** the door when you leave the room. You do not leave it open. The box is **shut**.

sing

When we **sing**, we use our voices to make music. The birds **sing** at sunrise. We **sang** carols at Christmas. Have you ever **sung** a song? Do you like **singing**?

Susan **sings** a sad song.

sink

If you drop a pebble into a pond, it will **sink** to the bottom. To **sink** means to drop down. The boat **sank** to the sea floor. The divers found a **sunken** ship. We washed the dishes in the **sink**. A **sink** is a basin for washing in the kitchen.

sister

A girl who has the same mother and father as you have is your **sister**.

six (6)

Six is the number that follows five. All insects have **six** legs.

size

Something's **size** tells you how big or small it is. You take a smaller **size** in shoes than I do.

skeleton

An animal's bones fit together to make its **skeleton**. Scientists have found very old **skeletons** of dinosaurs buried in rocks.

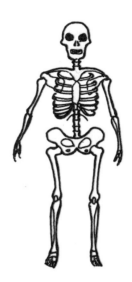

A human **skeleton** – you can see all the bones.

skirt

A **skirt** is often worn by women and girls. It is a piece of cloth that hangs from the waist. Some **skirts** can be long enough to reach the floor. Others can end above the knee.

sky

The **sky** is the open air above us. Today there are no clouds in the bright blue **sky**.

skyscraper

A **skyscraper** is a very tall building that reaches high into the sky. There are lots of **skyscrapers** in the city of New York.

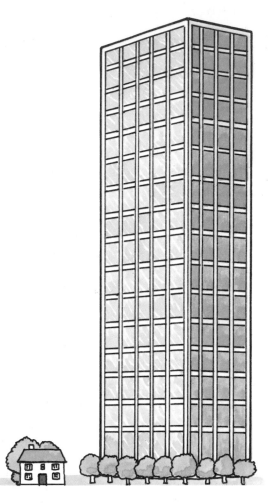

A tall **skyscraper** next to a small house.

slow

Anything **slow** does not move quickly. A snail moves very **slowly**.

small

A **small** thing is little. It is not big. A house is **smaller** than a skyscraper, but a box is the **smallest** of all.

smell

We **smell** with our noses. The flowers **smelled** sweet.

smile

You **smile** when there is a happy look on your face. You lift the corners of your mouth when you are **smiling**.

smoke

When things burn, they give off **smoke**. A gray cloud of **smoke** puffed up from the fire.

snail

A **snail** is a small animal with a hard shell on its back. **Snails** eat plants.

snake

A **snake** is a reptile. It has a long body and no legs. **Snakes** slide along the ground. Some **snakes** have a poisonous bite.

sneeze

People often **sneeze** when they have a cold. They make an "ah-choo" noise when air suddenly blows out of their mouth and nose.

snow

On very cold days, raindrops freeze into small white flakes that fall as **snow**. When **snow** falls in winter we throw **snowballs** and make a **snowman**.

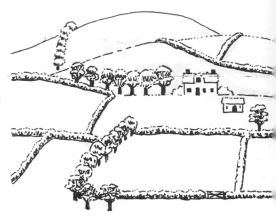

Snow lies over the countryside.

sofa

A **sofa** is a long seat. It has a back and arms and is soft to sit on. Our cat goes to sleep on the **sofa**.

This **sofa** is soft to sit on.

soft

Soft things are not hard or rough. Snow is **soft**. Silk is **soft**. Music is played **softly** when it is not loud.

78

soldier

A **soldier** is a person who belongs to the army. Sue and Tom gathered their toy **soldiers** for a battle.

something

The word **something** describes a thing that you don't know the name of. I thought she had **something** in her hand. I could not see what it was.

sometimes

Sometimes means not always. **Sometimes** I eat an apple for lunch. I get all my answers right **sometimes**.

son

Parents have a **son** if they have a male child.

song

A **song** is music for singing. **Songs** have words and music.

sound

You hear a **sound**. A police siren makes a very loud **sound**.

sour

Lemons taste **sour**. **Sour** is the opposite of sweet.

south

South is the direction opposite to north. Some birds fly **south** to warmer countries in the winter.

space

A **space** is a gap between things. Can you fill the **space** in this w rd? Beyond our earth there is **space**. **Spaceships** travel there.

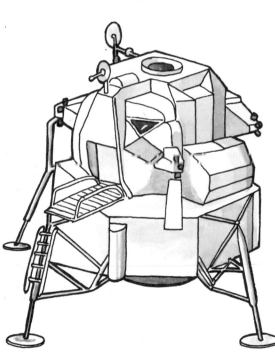

This **spacecraft** landed on the moon.

speak

When you say something you **speak**. Who is **speaking** on the radio? I have **spoken** to the teacher about your dancing lessons.

spell

1. You can **spell** words when you know which letters make them up.
2. Witches can make magic **spells** by saying the right words.

spend

1. You must **spend** your money if you want to buy anything. Have you **spent** much money?
2. To **spend** time means to pass time doing something. I **spent** a week at home when I had measles.

spider

A **spider** is a small animal with eight legs. It spins a web.

spin

1. To **spin** means to turn around and around. The laundry **spins** in the washing machine.
2. Cotton and wool are **spun** into strong threads. A spider **spins** thread from its body to make its web.

spoon

You use a **spoon** for eating. It has a handle and a bowl to scoop up food. You eat soup with a **spoon**.

spot

A **spot** is a small round mark or a location. My dog has **spots** on his nose. "X" marks the **spot** where the treasure is buried.

spring

1. **Spring** is the season of the year between winter and summer.
2. To **spring** means to jump up quickly.
3. A **spring** is a coil of wire that bounces up and down.

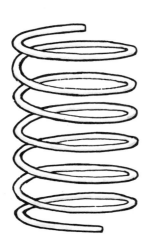

square

A **square** is a shape with four straight sides, all the same length. The band played in the town **square**.

squirrel

A **squirrel** is an animal with a bushy tail. **Squirrels** live in trees and eat mainly nuts.

The **squirrel** nibbles a nut.

stairs

Stairs are steps used for walking up and down. The children ran up the **staircase** to the room on the top floor.

stand

We **stand** on our feet. People were **standing** on the train because the seats were full. The horse **stood** very still.

star

A **star** is a distant sun that we see as a tiny bright light in the sky at night. **Stars** are far away from us in space.

start

We **start** when we begin. When I raise my arm you **start** the race. Have you **started** your homework?

steam

Steam is the gas made by boiling water. It rises in a cloud of white mist.

step

We take a **step** when we move a foot backward or forward.

sting

Bees and wasps can **sting** and so can the plants called nettles. I've been **stung**!

stomach

The **stomach** is the part of your body where your food goes after you eat. The food is mixed and softened in your **stomach**.

stone

Stones are pieces of rock. We use **stone** for building. **Gemstones** like rubies and emeralds are worth a lot of money.

stop

When you came to the end of what you are doing you **stop**. Ben **stopped** singing. **Stop** reading and put out the light.

stork

A **stork** is a large bird with long thin legs and a long thin beak. **Storks** live in marshy lands and eat insects, frogs, and snakes. They build big, untidy, nests.

storm

In a **storm** there is heavy rain with lightning and thunder. **Stormy** weather is rough and wet. The wind blows the sea into high waves during a **thunderstorm**.

A storm by the sea

strap

A **strap** is like a belt and is used to fasten a suitcase or a piece of clothing. **Straps** have buckles. The **strap** on my schoolbag has broken.

strawberry

A **strawberry** is a soft red fruit that grows in the summer. We eat **strawberries** with cream.

street

A **street** is a road in a town. There are houses and shops on High **Street**.

stretch

Some things will **stretch** out longer if you pull them. Elastic **stretches**. When I **stretch** I reach out. I **stretched** out my arm to pick the biggest apple off the tree.

string

String is a thick thread that we use to tie things.

stripe

A **stripe** is a long thin line. A zebra is an animal with black and white **stripes**.

strong

Strong things are powerful. Strong people can lift heavy weights. Fish has a **strong** smell.

subtract

To **subtract** means to take away. What is two **subtracted** from seven?

sugar

We add **sugar** to our food to make it taste sweet. I put **sugar** on my cornflakes.

sum

When you add numbers together you find the total **sum**. What is the **sum** of two plus seven?

summer

Summer is the season of the year between spring and fall. We take our vacations in **summer** when the weather is warm and sunny.

In **summer** it is sometimes hot and sunny.

sun

The **sun** shines in the sky. Its burning gases heat and light the earth.

supermarket

A **supermarket** is a large store. You can help yourself to all the things on sale in a **supermarket**, but be sure to pay for them at the checkout counter!

sunflower

The **sunflower** plant grows very tall and has a big yellow flower. We get oil from **sunflower** seeds.

surprise

A **surprise** is not expected. I didn't know about my birthday party. It was a **surprise**.

swallow

When you let food or drink go down your throat you **swallow**.

A **swallow** flies to its nest.

swan

A **swan** is a big white bird with a long neck. **Swans** live on water. A baby **swan** is a cygnet.

sweep

We **sweep** the floor with a broom to brush away the dust.

sweet

Sweet things are not sour. Candy is **sweet**?

swim

Animals **swim** through water. You **swim** by pushing forward with your arms and legs. Jill is a good **swimmer**. She **swam** all around the rocks.

Stephen **swims** in the swimming pool.

swing

You can **swing** from side to side, or backward and forward. The acrobat is **swinging** from the trapeze. He **swung** high above the crowd.

table

A **table** is a piece of furniture. A **tabletop** is a flat surface to put things on.

tail

Lots of animals have **tails**. Dogs wag their **tails**. The **tail** is the end of the animal's backbone that sticks out.

take

Take this cup. Hold it in your hands. Now **take** it into the kitchen, please. She was **taking** the dog for a walk. Dan **took** his coat to the car. I have **taken** my model car to school.

talk

To **talk** is to speak words to each other. Only people **talk**. The sisters **talked** for hours.

tall

A giraffe is **tall**. Its head is a long way from the ground. A pine tree is **taller** than a giraffe.

Tank

A **tank** carries soldiers into battle. **Tanks** have big guns and thick armor.

Tanks have powerful guns and strong armor.

taste

Taste tells us what we are eating. Sugar has a sweet **taste**. Lemons have a sour **taste**. You **taste** food with your tongue.

tea

The **tea** we drink is made from the leaves of the **tea** plant. The farms where **tea** is grown are called **tea** plantations.

teach

Anyone who shows you how to do something is **teaching** you. At school **teachers** **teach** lots of things. My **teacher** **taught** me to write in French.

The **teacher** helps the pupil.

team

A group of people playing a game together make a **team**. The two **teams** played football.

tear (rhymes with hair)

When you **tear** something, you rip or break it. I **tore** my shirt on a nail.

tear (rhymes with fear)

A **tear** is a drop of water that runs from your eye when you cry. Wipe your **tears** with this tissue.

telephone

The **telephone** carries your voice through wires to another person far away. The sound of your voice is carried to the other person by electric signals.

television

Television brings moving pictures and sounds into our homes. Inside the **television** is a special tube. The programs we watch come from a **TV** station.

tell

When you **tell** someone your name, you say it to them. **Tell** me another story. I liked the story you **told** me yesterday.

temperature

The **temperature** of a thing is how hot or cold it is. When there is ice and snow, the **temperature** is low. Metals melt at very high **temperatures**.

temple

A **temple** is a place where people go to worship God.

ten (10)

Ten is the number after nine. You have **ten** fingers and **ten** toes.

tennis

When you play **tennis**, you hit a ball over a net with a **tennis** raquet. **Tennis** is played on a **tennis** court.

Tina and Trevor are playing **tennis**.

test

To **test** a thing means to try it out. The men **tested** the machine to see if it worked. We had a spelling **test**. The teacher asked us to spell words.

the

The is used before the name of a thing. **The** house was on top of **the** hill.

then

Then tells us something happened next. First I brushed my teeth, **then** I went to bed.

there

There tells us about a place. My shoes are **there**. **There** is a spider in the bathtub.

A **thermometer** is filled with mercury.

thermometer

A **thermometer** measures temperature. It tell us how hot or cold things are. The nurse put a **thermometer** in my mouth.

thick

A **thick** sweater keeps you warm. Animals with **thick** coats have a lot of hair. The snow was **thick**. It covered everything.

thin

A **thin** thing is not thick. A sheet of paper is **thin**. A fat person is not **thin**.

think

When you **think,** you are using your brain. Jane was **thinking** about her homework. I **thought** I knew the answers.

thirsty

When we need a drink, we feel **thirsty.** Playing in hot sun makes you **thirsty**.

three (3)

Three is the number after two. A cycle with **three** wheels is called a tricycle.

throat

Your **throat** is in your neck. It is hard to swallow with a sore **throat**.

A **tiger** has stripes.

thumb

Your **thumb** is the thick, short finger on the inside of your hand. You hold a pencil between your index finger and **thumb**.

thunder

Thunder is the loud rumbling noise we often hear during a storm. **Thunder** comes after lightning.

tidy

Tidy means neat, clean, and in order. Jan is very **tidy**. She puts everything away in its place.

tie

We **tie** string round packages to fasten them. We **tie** a knot in the string. Dad wore a bow **tie** to the party. He **tied** it around his neck. We are **tying** a label on the bag.

tiger

A **tiger** is a large wild animal of the cat family. Its fur has black and yellow stripes.

tight

Something that is **tight** is not loose. My shoes were so **tight** that they hurt my feet.

time

We measure **time** in hours and minutes. It is **time** to go to bed. Will you be a long **time** in the store?

tiny

Tiny means very small. A snail is a **tiny** animal. A fly is **tinier**.

tired

You feel **tired** when you need a rest. Joe felt **tired** after he climbed the hill. I'm **tired** of doing homework. You may find things **tiring** if they go on for a long time.

toe

Your ten **toes** are at the end of your feet.

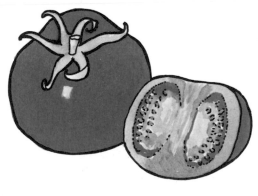

tomato

A **tomato** is a soft red fruit. We often have **tomatoes** in a salad.

tongue

You can move your **tongue** inside your mouth. It is the long soft part that helps you talk and taste. Cats drink milk with their **tongues**.

tool

A **tool** helps us to do work. Hammers and saws are **tools** we use for woodwork.

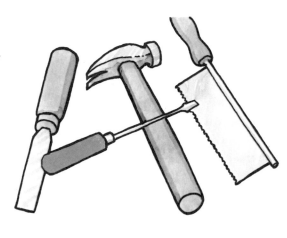

Can you name these **tools**?

tooth

A **tooth** is used for biting and chewing. Your **teeth** grow in your gums.

A tractor plows the field.

top

The **top** is the highest part of anything. The roof is the **top** of a house.

touch

To **touch** means to feel something with your hand. Close your eyes and **touch** your nose. Yesterday I **touched** my friend's cat.

towel

Jane dried herself with a **towel** after her bath. Towels are cloths that soak up water.

tower

A **tower** is a tall building or part of a building. The Leaning **Tower** of Pisa may fall down one day.

tractor

A farmer drives a **tractor** in the fields. A **tractor** can pull heavy loads. It has huge wheels to help it move through the mud.

traffic

The cars and trucks that move on the road make up **traffic**. All the **traffic** must stop at a red **traffic** light.

train

A **train** is pulled along a track by an engine. Behind comes a line of coaches.

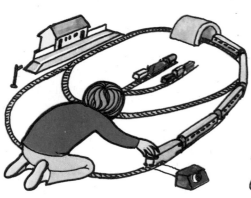

travel

When we go from one place to another, we **travel**. They **traveled** abroad for their vaction. My friend is a great **traveler**. She likes **traveling**.

trawler

Some fishing boats drag a net behind them under the sea. They are **trawlers**. They **trawl** the seabed for fish.

tread

To step or walk on. She heard the **tread** of feet. The mark of a footprint. The pattern of grooves cut in the face of a car tire.

treasure

We pretended to be pirates looking for buried **treasure** of silver and gold. Things of great value are **treasured**.

The chest is full of **treasure**.

tree

A **tree** is a tall plant with a trunk, branches, and leaves. Many **trees** growing together are called a forest.

triangle

A shape with three straight sides is a **triangle**.

truck

A **truck** moves on wheels. It carries heavy loads along the roads.

true

If something is true it is right. You tell the **truth** when you say what really happened. Are you always **truthful**?

try

I **try** to bake a cake. You find out if you can do something by **trying**. The man **tried** to mend the engine. I am **trying** on this sweater to see if it fits.

tunnel

A **tunnel** is a hole made under the ground. A mole **tunnels** through the earth. We drove in a **tunnel** under the river.

turn

To **turn** is to go around. The wheels **turn** to make the bicycle move along.

turtle

Turtles have hard shells and often live in water.

two (2)

Two is the number after one. You have two hands and two feet.

typewriter

We press the keys of a **typewriter** to make it print letters.

A **typewriter** is used by a typist.

ugly

Ugly things are not pretty to look at. The **ugly** sisters were cruel to Cinderella.

umbrella

You hold an **umbrella** over your head to keep off the rain. An **umbrella** is a frame covered with material.

uncle

I have three **uncles**. One is my mother's brother. One is my father's brother. The third **uncle** is married to the aunt who is my father's sister.

under

Anything below or beneath something else is **under** it. The road passes **under** the bridge.

understand

Can you **understand** what you are reading? Do you know what the words mean? If you **understand** you know about what you are doing, or the words you are hearing. I **understood** what the Frenchman said.

unhappy

You feel sad when you are **unhappy**. Grandma cried because she was so **unhappy**.

unicorn

A **unicorn** is a make-believe animal from fairy tales. A white horse with one horn in its forehead is a **unicorn**.

uniform

A **uniform** is a special suit of clothing. Nurses wear **uniforms**; so do police officers.

untidy

When things are scattered abut all over the place, they look **untidy**. My brother's room always looks **untidy**.

up

To go **up** means to go higher. I went **up** the stairs. I sent my balloon **up** in the air.

upside-down

Something is **upside-down** when its top is where the bottom should be. Turn the bottle **upside-down** to pour out the sauce.

upstairs

The parts of a building above the bottom floor are **upstairs**. My bedroom is downstairs but John goes **upstairs** to bed.

use

Things that we can **use** are **useful**. We **use** a mug to drink out of. A broken mug is of no **use**. Broken tools are **useless**.

usually

Things **usually** happen when they happen most of the time. I **usually** get up early.

valley

A **valley** is the low ground between two high hills. We saw the village in the **valley** from the hill above.

van

A **van** is a small covered truck for carrying loads.

vegetable

We cook and eat plants called **vegetables**. A carrot is a **vegetable**, and so is a cabbage.

Try to name these **vegetables**.

very

The wind was **very** cold. It was colder than usual. The teacher was **very** cross. He was especially angry.

violin

The **violin** is a musical instrument with four strings. People who play **violins** are called **violinists**. They pull a stick called a bow across the tight strings to make different sounds.

Valerie plays the **violin**.

visit

You **visit** when you go to see something. We **visited** the zoo last week. How many **visitors** came here yesterday?

voice

Your **voice** makes sounds when you speak or sing. The singer had a deep **voice**. Dick whispered in a soft **voice**.

volcano

Melted rock and gas from inside the earth push their way out through a **volcano** when it erupts.

vulture

A **vulture** is a large bird that feeds off the remains of dead animals.

wait

I am **waiting** for my friend. I will stay here until he comes. We all waited at the bus stop. The **waiter** brought our food.

wake

We **wake** after a sleep. The birds **woke** up early this morning.

walk

We **walk** as we put one foot in front of another to move along the ground. She is **walking** to school today. Let's go for a **walk**. We **walked** all the way to town. We are good **walkers**.

wall

A **wall** is built with bricks or stones. A house usually has four **walls**. We decorate **walls** with **wallpaper**. The Romans built a high **wall** between England and Scotland. It is named Hadrian's **Wall** after the emperor who had it built.

want

To **want** is to need or wish for something you haven't got. Joe **wants** a violin. He has **wanted** one for a long time.

war

There is a **war** when countries fight each other. Many people were killed in World **War** II.

warm

When you feel **warm** you feel fairly hot. It was **warm** in the sun. A fire gives us **warmth**. **Warm** your socks on the radiator.

wash

We **wash** things with water to get them clean. It is best to use soap for **washing**. Have you **washed** behind your ears?

wasp

A **wasp** is a flying insect that is much like a bee. **Wasps** make a buzzing noise as they fly and can sting to protect themselves. **Wasps** live in nests.

waste

We **waste** things that can't be used. We **waste** food we cannot eat. Don't **waste** time doing nothing!

watch

1. To **watch** means to look at or look after for a time. I would like to **watch** a film. **Watch** my bicycle while I'm away.
2. We wear a **watch** to tell the time. Some **watches** give the date as well.

What is the time by this **watch**?

water

Water is a liquid that has no color. It falls as rain to fill the rivers, lakes, and oceans. We drink **water** and use it for washing.

Water from a river falls over rocks and this makes a **waterfall**.

wave

1. The wind makes **waves** as it blows across the surface of the sea. A huge **wave** crashed against the shore.
2. We **waved** our hands from side to side to say goodbye to Dad.

89

wear

We **wear** clothes on our bodies. Pat is **wearing** a very bright sweater. Has she **worn** it before? Clothes that are **worn** a lot will **wear** out. The elbows on your old jacket are very **worn**. I **wore** my jeans yesterday.

weather

When it rains or snows, we say the **weather** is bad. When the sun shines, we have good **weather**. The sailors listened to the **weather** report on the radio before setting out to sea.

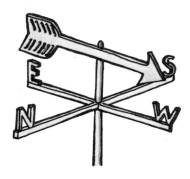

web

A spider spins a net called a **web** and uses it to catch flies.

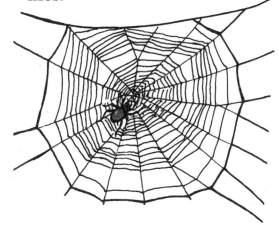

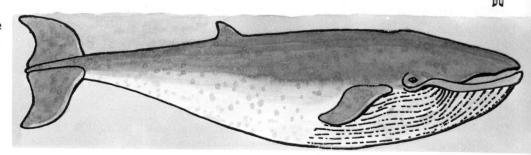

The biggest animal is a **whale**.

weigh

We **weigh** things to see how heavy they are. The woman in the store **weighed** the candies we bought. Can you guess the **weight** of the cake? Astronauts in space are **weightless**. They float around in their spacecraft.

well

1. A **well** is a hole that is dug deep into the ground. They dig **wells** through rock to find oil or water.
2. **Well** also means feeling good. Are you feeling **well** again after your illness? How **well** did you do in your tests?

west

West is the direction that is opposite to east. The sun sets in the **western** sky each evening.

wet

Things are **wet** when they are not dry. Jack stood in the rain and got **wet**.

whale

The **whale** is the biggest animal of all. Whales live in the sea. A baby blue **whale** is bigger than a grown elephant when it is born!

what

You ask the question **what** if you want to find out something. **What** do you want? **What** are you doing?

wheat

Wheat is a grass crop that is grown by farmers. **Wheat** seeds are crushed into flour to make bread.

wheel

A round **wheel** turns on its center. Trucks, trains, and other vehicles move on **wheels**.

when

The question **when** asks about the time that something happened. **When** did you last see the glove that you lost? **When** also tells you the time that something happens. We were pleased **when** our team won the cup.

where

Where asks a question or tells you about a place. **Where** did Jenny hide her book? The onions came up **where** I planted them.

which

The question **which** asks about two or more things or people. **Which** jar holds the most candies? **Which** boy is the smallest?

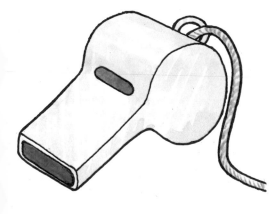

A **whistle** makes a loud noise.

whistle

Blow through your lips to make a **whistle**. The man was **whistling** to his dog. The referee blew his **whistle** at the end of the game.

who

Who asks a question about people. **Who** was he?

whole

The boy weeded the **whole** garden, not just a part of it. I read the **whole** book in three hours.

why

We ask the question **why** when we want to know the reason that something happened. **Why** did the girl run away? **Why** are you standing on my toe?

wide

The space from one side to another tells you how **wide** it is. How **wide** is the Atlantic Ocean? I want you to stand with your legs **wide** apart. The distance across is called the **width**.

wigwam

The Indians in America lived in tents or huts called **wigwams**. We made a **wigwam** from an old sheet.

wild

Wild animals are not tame. They live away from people and find their own food. The lions in Africa are big **wild** cats. The cats that live with us at home are tame. Plants that have not been put in the ground by humans are **wild** plants. Animals that live in the **wild** learn to look after themselves.

win

When you **win**, you beat all the other people in a race or competition. Who is **winning** the game? Have we **won** the match?

wind

When air moves it makes a **wind**. A strong **wind** is called a gale or hurricane. Our fence blew down on a **windy** night.

wing

Animals have **wings** to help them fly. Airplanes also have **wings** to keep them up in the air.

winter

Winter is the season of the year between fall and spring. **Winter** days are short and cold.

wipe

You **wipe** things dry or clean by rubbing them with a cloth. **Wipe** your hands dry after you wash.

wire

A **wire** is a long thin piece of metal. Electricity comes to your house along **wires**.

wish

We **wish** for things we don't have. He **wished** he had a dog.

with

Two or more things together are **with** each other. Bill went **with** his sister to the park. They went **without** their brothers. **Without** is the opposite of **with**. If you are **without** something you don't have it.

woman

An adult female person is a **woman**. Girls become **women** when they grow up.

wood

Wood is the hard part of a tree. A group of trees is sometimes called a **wood**. **Wooden** furniture is made from trees.

wool

Wool is sheep's hair. A sheep's coat is cut off every year and made into a fine thread. Jane knitted her sweater with red **wool**.

word

Letters are put together to make **words**. The letters "d" "o" and "g" can be used to make the **word** "dog."

work

We **work** at a job. My mom **works** in a store. I like **working** in the garden. Let's finish our **homework** and then we can go out.

worm

A **worm** is a long thin animal without legs. It lives underground or in water. Birds eat **worms**.

wrist (rist)

Your **wrist** joins your arm to your hand. You wear a watch on your **wrist**. Your **wrist** bends.

write

We **write** when we use a pen or pencil to make words on paper. I am **writing** a letter. Have you **written** to your aunt? Yes, I **wrote** yesterday.

X ray

The doctor at the hospital took an **X ray** of my broken arm. An **X ray** is a special kind of wave. Machines using **X rays** take pictures of the bones in your body.

xylophone (zy-le-fone)

A **xylophone** is a musical instrument with bars made of flat pieces of metal or wood. When you hit the bars, they make a sound.

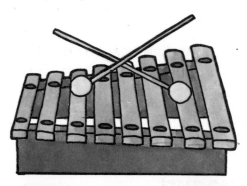

yacht (yot)

A **yacht** is a large sailboat. We race model **yachts** on the lake.

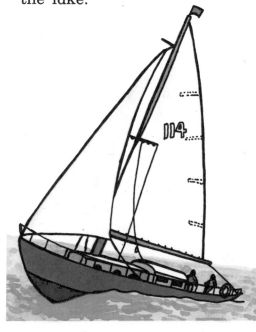

yawn

When we are tired, our mouths stretch open wide and we breathe in deeply. Other people may start **yawning** too.

year

A **year** lasts twelve months. We all have birthdays once a **year**. Every fourth **year** is a leap **year**. It has 366 days instead of the usual 365.

yogurt

Yogurt is a food made from sour milk. I like **yogurt** mixed with strawberries.

yolk

The yellow part of an egg is the **yolk**. I like to cook eggs so that the **yolk** is soft, not hard.

young

You are **young** now, but your grandparents may be old. **Youngsters** are not yet grown up. When animals have **young**, they take good care of their babies.

zebra

A **zebra** is a animal like a wild horse. Its coat has black and white stripes. **Zebras** come from Africa.

zero (0)

Zero is another name for nothing. In winter, some places have a temperature that falls below **zero**. That's very cold!

zigzag

A **zigzag** is not a straight line. It turns sharply out and in again. Betty ran down the street in a **zigzag**.

zipper

A **zipper** is a metal fastener with teeth that grip together. Many skirts and pants are fastened with a **zipper**.

zoo

Lots of wild animals are kept at the **zoo**.